BULLIED

Fig. 1. Hieronymus Bosch, *Ship of Fools* (1490–1500)

First published in 2021 by punctum books, Earth, Milky Way.
https://punctumbooks.com

ISBN-13: 978-1-953035-72-1 (print)
ISBN-13: 978-1-953035-73-8 (ePDF)

DOI: 10.53288/0320.1.00

LCCN: 2021947619
Library of Congress Cataloging Data is available from the Library of Congress

Book design: Vincent W.J. van Gerven Oei
Cover image: Jonathan Alexander

spontaneous acts of scholarly combustion

HIC SVNT MONSTRA

Jonathan Alexander

The Story of an Abuse

p.

Contents

Acknowledgments

First and foremost, I thank Eileen A. Fradenburg Joy and Vincent W.J. van Gerven Oei, co-directors of punctum books, for their support and enthusiasm for this second book. After the publication of *Creep*, I knew that I wanted Eileen and Vincent to shepherd this new effort to publication. I am forever in their debt.

And I'm in the debt of many others, friends and colleagues, fellow writers, those who have thought and fought with me over the years about abuse, sexuality, autofiction, autotheory, and other related, relevant, and random topics: Karen Yescavage, Jackie Rhodes, Sherryl Vint, David Lumb, David Wallace, Michelle Latiolais, Dillon Sefic, Jack Miles, Julietta Singh, Richard Godden, Rhian Hughes, Nasrin Rahimieh, George Lang, and Susan C. Jarratt. At the *Los Angeles Review of Books*, Tom Lutz, Boris Dralyuk, Medaya Ocher, and Eric Newman have been invaluable editors and co-conspirators; I thank *LARB* in particular for publishing earlier versions of some passages in this book.

And finally, always, Mack and Mother, my most immediate family, who with our cat, Cooper, heal so much that has been wrong. I can only hope that I heal something in them too, and, if I don't, then I will always be grateful for what they so generously give, what they so blessedly make possible in my life.

Preface

In 2017, I published *Creep: A Life, a Theory, an Apology*, a book I called a "critical memoir," mixing personal narrative, textual analysis, and theoretical speculation to describe how, as a young queer person growing up in the Deep South in the 1970s and '80s, I had come to understand myself as, essentially, a "creep," as someone whose desires and interests, whose very being was creepy. I had been hailed, in the Althusserian sense, as a "creep," and I heeded the call, internalizing homophobia — from people and from institutions, such as schools and religions, as well as the mass media response to the AIDS epidemic — as a deeply felt sense of personal creepiness, and a creepiness easily detectable by others around me.

Past generations of queer folks might have been interpellated as "criminal" or "pathological," psychologically diseased. Edmund White's autofictional account of growing up queerly in the '50s and '60s, *The Beautiful Room Is Empty*, features a narrator whose self-descriptions, whose very personal language of self, is laced with dual discourses of the criminal and the pathological. I didn't quite feel criminal and pathological. Not quite. But how *did* I feel? I wanted to write a book that spoke to the shift in discourses of subjective interpellation that accounted for concomitant shifts in how our culture understands and talks about queerness — shifts that were slowly shedding the criminal and the pathological but that were still not accepting or even tolerant, and that, especially with the onset of the AIDS epidemic, re-tained a sense of deep dis-ease. Discourses of creepiness — that which still lurks in the shadows, full of hidden intention and vaguely menacing — were the ones I grow up with, that circu-lated liberally whenever queerness was spoken about. They are the discourses that seemed to "fit."

Of course, I'm talking about a specific time and place, and I also wanted to try to account for the different temporal and spatial distributions of these discourses. While some urban centers on the coasts were moving from pathology to creepi-ness to even a kind of acceptance of the "alternative" when talk-ing about queerness, my experience of the Deep South under Ronald Regan was stuck somewhere between criminality (quite literally in the last days of the "Crimes against Nature" laws) and the still partially unspeakable, or that which could only be spoken of with great discomfort.

Creep, as such, is a very personal book, focusing on interior experience. This book is quite personal too. But the valence in *Bullied* is different. In this book, I have attempted to turn from the personal to the institutional, moving the center of gravity of my writing toward a description and analysis of the kinds of structures that interpellate queer subjects, and to the domains that generate and disseminate the kinds of discourses that make queer lives unsustainable, that damage them, and that even kill them. So, in *Bullied,* I talk more explicitly about experi-ences of Church and State, but also the media through which I learned — and through which queers continue to learn — about their social positioning, their status, their desirability (or lack thereof) in our culture. Indeed, the position of queerness in the larger culture, despite gay marriage and the repeal of "Don't Ask, Don't Tell," remains uneven, contested, vexed, and damag-ing, still, in many quarters. As I write this, in the social isolation mandated by the spread of the novel coronavirus, I read reports of elected officials, church leaders, and others who blame the spread of the virus on queer people. So, while continuing to tell my own story of being bullied and abused, I offer reflections on contemporary subjects as varied as Jussie Smollett, drug abuse, MAGA-capped boys, sadomasochism, Larry Nassar, Catholic priests, and gay cruising. Throughout, I consider how my inter-pellation of "creepiness" was achieved in large part through bul-lying, sometimes directed at me personally but more often than not just a set of discourses and practices that formed part of the general anti-queer landscape through which I found — and nearly lost — myself. That kind of interpellation — that kind of bullying — continues for many, many people.

In the process, I also recount — and confront — a painful di-mension of my own self-narration. I describe how, as a young man, I struggled with the realization that the story I had been telling myself about being abused by a favorite uncle as a child might actually just have been a "story" — a story I told myself and others to justify both my lifelong struggle with anxiety and to explain my attraction to other men — that is, to understand my creepiness, and even to *battle* my queerness. Now, a man in middle age, having largely accepted my queerness, I ask myself some difficult questions: What happens when what you thought was the defining moment of your life might be a figment of your imagination? How do you understand — and live with — defini-tive feelings of having been abused, when the origin of those feelings won't adhere to a singular event but are rather diffused across years of experience, years of being bullied?

To approach such questions, I generally eschew psychologiz-ing discourses because those were not ones I had much access to, except in one particular case which I recount. Instead, I try to answer these questions by telling my story and by listening carefully to the stories that are told about queerness in the world around me — then and now. I turn a critical eye on the story that I told myself when I was a young man, the story of my abuse. "Story" though it was, I maintain that some form of abuse did occur. Ultimately, then, *Bullied* is about what it means to suffer abuse when such is spread across multiple actors and locales, implicating a family, a school, a culture, and a politics — as op-posed to a singular individual who just happened to be the only openly gay man in my young life.

PART ONE

Scenes from Childhood

I'm in my mid-twenties, talking on the phone with the woman I will soon be marrying. I'm finishing up my PhD and am what we used to call in the Deep South "dirt poor." Well, for the last four years, not quite dirt poor—I've been on a teaching assistantship, which pays better than many jobs back home. I've been reading and writing double-time because my funding only lasts four years, and I need to finish the degree. We don't take out loans where I come from, not for things like a degree in the humanities. I finish the PhD in four years—rather than the normal eight or more—not because I'm particularly intelligent; I'm just dogged and afraid. I am driven. Demons at the door, demons inside. It was time to move on.

Already I'm not talking about what I want to talk about. Work obsesses me. For decades, it's practically all I can talk about. But now I want to write about my *it*. Not talk about it, but write. A therapist or two has heard me say something about this. But otherwise I've never used the word "abuse" to talk about my first sexual experiences. Now I will.

***

I'm talking to the woman who will soon be my wife, right after we both finish our graduate degrees, on the single pay phone in my apartment complex. It's the 1980s so no one I know has a cell phone. I wait till late in the evening when I hope there will be fewer people around. She's in Boston and we talk every week, usually on a Thursday night. I'll head from Baton Rouge to New Orleans on Friday to work over the weekend, playing piano for a small Baptist church.

As I talk to my soon-to-be wife, the movie of my abuse plays in the back of my mind. I'm not talking about it with her. I'm thinking about it. I see a murky blue background, movement obscured, maybe bodies writhing, bodies moving around. Something is happening. I hear a piano playing over the pulsating or palpitating blue field. Something vaguely classical. Chopin? No, I heard Chopin during the opening credits of some art film that I went to see with the older woman that I was in love with a few years back. I don't remember the name of the film but the idea of painfully yearning piano music playing over a film's credits has stayed with me for decades now as the height of indie film scoring.

But this isn't an indie film. It's the story of my abuse. That's what this film, this story, is supposedly about. My uncle, when I was a child, sexually abused me. I was the victim of childhood sexual abuse. He was in his thirties. He died when I was twelve and he was forty-one. Cancer. Though some of his siblings, god-fearing Cajun folk (or at least neighbor-fearing — definitely neighbor-fearing), thought he might have contracted AIDS in the French Quarter. He was gay.

(I do not have AIDS, but I will worry about it — about it and many, many other things, for some time. I have been tested for it a few times, but I only ever worried once. Years ago, actually probably not long after this phone conversation, right before I was about to be married.)

The movie of what is not yet my abuse is starting again in my head. Only ever starting. I never imagine further than the opening, with the yearning romantic piano and the shifting blue field obscuring the bodies beneath. And I never see beyond these credits, which I can't even quite read. Or even the title.

Years from this moment, literally decades, I'll wake up from a dream in which an academic colleague and I (work obsessed) will be waiting outside the doors of a theater. Perhaps I'm getting popcorn, I don't know who's waiting for whom, but we are about to go see a film called WE ARE ONLY. Just like that. ALL CAPS. WE ARE ONLY. I want to see this film. I have no idea what it's about. Actually, I think I might want to write this film, or make the poster for it. The title of the film, WE ARE ONLY, in very visible letters, runs along the bottom. There's other script but it's indistinct, maybe indecipherable, so we don't know who made the film, who wrote the screenplay, who directed it, what company made it, what art house distributed it. This is an indie film after all. Very independent. I want to write this film, but I don't make films. I want to write a book called WE ARE ONLY.

No, not quite right. *We Are Only.* I think I like that better.

* * *

Here's a reality. I'm sitting with my mother and father, just days before I'm to be married. I'm 25. I have finished work on my PhD in comparative literature. Part of me is looking forward to starting my life, starting a life, a kind of life that I think I should have, that I think I should want. I'm sitting with my mother and father, talking about the upcoming ceremony, and I start crying, then sobbing. I'm sobbing. They want to know what's wrong. It isn't a question anymore, but a statement. They are not asking what's wrong. They are saying something is wrong.

And I can identify what, actually, is wrong.

But my father beats me to the punch. My father, who otherwise took next to no interest in me, the man who likely didn't even want me to be born, or who actually suspected that I might not be his own child because he didn't want me that much, thinks he knows what's wrong.

"I think I know what it is. You're a homosexual."

I'm writing this sitting in a coffeeshop, tapping away on my laptop, writing, writing, and looking up to check out the cute barista, the boy who doesn't mind flirting a little bit, the college kid at the school down the road, today wearing cute little densely patterned socks sneaking out beneath the rolled ankle cuffs of his jeans. I've never seen him without his jaunty baseball cap. I wonder what his hair is like, his black hair.

My uncle had black hair.

I return to my father, the man who didn't want me, offering me one of the truths of my life. *You are a homosexual.*

"Well, you're close, I said. "I think I was molested by Uncle Glen, and it's given me these thoughts, these feelings…I don't know what to do."

That was as close as I could get to the truth at the time.

My parents don't seem that surprised. I was always a weird child, introverted, bookish. Bullied. A target. Called fag, faggot, gay, queer, homo — constantly, incessantly. How can so many people be wrong? I was otherwise good, a churchgoer, a good boy, a good boy. But quiet, shy, bookish, more comfortable with my books, my classical music, than other people, other boys, other men my own age.

I desperately did not want to be gay.

That became the organizing truth of my twenties, in south Louisiana, in the early '90s. How do you deal with such a truth at such a time, in such a place? You find a backstory. In my case, I *knew* the backstory. I was convinced of it. I was molested by my uncle as a child, the only uncle I really knew, my mother's brother, who had moved to New Orleans with her when they were just children. He was gay. He had a partner. We grew up knowing him and Michael, before he died of cancer when I was just a kid, 12 or so, as I was entering puberty myself, just on the verge of having my first thoughts, my first sexual thoughts, *bad thoughts,* about other boys. Right when the bullying became intense, severe, terrifying. Terror. Bullying is terror. Some kids protect themselves from their own thoughts by torturing others. Some other kids are the terrorized, the tortured.

Sitting with my mother and the father who didn't want me, I talk about a night I barely remember, so many years ago, a night when Uncle Glen had taken me to see *Fantasia*. He loved classical music. He was a big man, burly, strong. He took me to this film. I was maybe six, or seven. Young. Maybe younger. My mother and my father start talking about how I had called them that night, wanting to be picked up, *pick me up please,* that I wanted to go home, but they didn't come get me, they were having a night out, whatever, their own private time. I don't remember any of that, but I remember the film, bits and pieces of the film, something blue, but immediately, in that moment, sitting with my parents, sobbing, I'm wondering, *why didn't you get me, why didn't you get me?* He was molesting me. I was being molested.

I don't know what my parents were thinking, except likely what I was thinking: that this explains so much. This explains *everything.* This is why I'm having the feelings about other boys that I've had, this is what people can read in my presence so clearly, this is why I am called out as a fag, faggot, gay, queer, homo. It's not my fault. It's not my fault. We are confident, even

23

relieved. My sobbing calms us all. I can go through with this. I can go through with getting married. It's all going to be ok.

I was confident I had been molested. I don't remember being molested.

***

When Alice Sebold writes about her rape in *Lucky*, she offers us the horror up front, in her first chapter. She was clearly violated, raped. But wait — the passive voice doesn't do justice to her description. *Someone raped her.* Her description merits the active voice: "When I came to, I knew I was staring up into the eyes of the man who would kill me. At that moment I signed myself over to him. I was convinced that I would not live." But then, given the momentousness of the experience, the near totality that it comes to assume in one's life — "My life was over; my life had just begun" — the passive creeps back in to signal the *fait accompli,* the grounding incident against which all subsequent experiences, thoughts, feelings, and actions are measured: "When I was raped I lost my virginity and almost lost my life. I also discarded certain assumptions I had held about how the world worked and about how safe I was."[1]

My question in this book, the one I'm writing, is simple: what happens if the totalizing event, the traumatic occurrence, is one you *think* might have happened, but maybe didn't? This question has structured my life. I experienced a trauma. I believed for a long time it was a childhood sexual abuse. It may not have occurred. But I still am left with the experience of having been abused. I believe I was abused.

Again, the passive voice, a diffusion of agency. And that might be the most appropriate way to characterize my experience of abuse, a diffusion of agency and more: a saturation of the world around me with threat, threat manifest at times, then slithering back into ambience, a background of hostility, a ceaseless potential for the inflicting of pain, an ever-present potential, now deeply internalized as fear.

***

---

1   Alice Sebold's *Lucky,* published by Charles Scribner's Sons in 1999, is well worth the read, even if I differentiate what I'm doing in this book from what Sebold is doing in hers.

I had been raised (the passive voice again) in a culture heavily influenced by catholicism, in south Louisiana, my teachers priests and nuns, and then brothers running the all-boys high school I was sent to in order to escape the sketchy public schools, my family part of white flight and the reinforcement of racialized economic lines even in the 1980s, long after the supposed "integration" of schools. One could choose not to integrate, if you could afford it, and while my parents weren't rich, having clawed their way from the working class into the lower middle class, they still set aside money for what we called "parochial" education — private and religious. Since I was never baptized catholic, I never took communion, much less went to confession (what would *that* have been like?), but I went to many, many masses, even played the piano to accompany the off-key singing of some of the brothers. *And he will raise you up on eagle's wings, bear you on the breath of life...* I may be misremembering these lines. What does it mean to be borne aloft on a breath of life, that breath, the breath of God apparently, supporting the wings of the eagle, the animal to which you are compared, the animal soaring higher and higher? Here the metaphor breaks down for me, the eagle circling, circling, high in the air, anticipating the dive down to slaughter. I am borne up to slaughter? I don't understand, I don't understand the metaphor. I am not catholic.

***

I'm writing this when the news is flooded with images and reports of a group of teen boys from Covington Catholic High School in a standoff with an Indigenous elder, steadily banging his drum during the 2019 Indigenous Peoples March in Washington, DC.[2] The boys were on a trip to the capital to participate in a March for Life rally and were visiting the Lincoln Memorial. The encounter wasn't planned, but the images and videos, which went viral as we say, infecting how we perceive the world around us, show the boys, one in particular wearing a MAGA cap, seeming to mimic and attempting to stare down an Indigenous man in his sixties. It's a creepy video. What are these kids thinking? And the one face-to-face with the elder, not backing down, not moving out of the way, seemingly in a staring contest — what's going through his mind?

As more of the story came out, we learned that the catholic schoolboys had just been accosted by a group of Black men, Hebrew Israelites, who were apparently casting aspersions on pretty much everyone around them, calling the boys bigots and faggots. The boys kept their cool. When the Indigenous elder, a man named Nathan Phillips, started beating his drum, he was trying to intervene, sending out a prayer, stepping in to avert potential conflict. The boy he stands toe-to-toe with was, as the boy reported, also trying to keep his cool, thinking the best thing to do was not react but smile calmly in the face of an escalating situation. That larger story slowly came out, but not before the initial video — of the MAGA-capped boy and the Indigenous Philips in a standoff — circulated everywhere, epitomizing for many the kinds of white, privileged, and racist contempt for minorities that has come to characterize the white far right.

I can't know the full — and certainly complex — story here, what actually happened on that day outside the Lincoln Memorial. But I found those initial videos of the standoff, as we say these days, triggering. I immediately felt cast back to my own catholic all-boys high school days, surrounded by other white, middle-class boys, full of their straight privilege, and knowing

---

2   There are many accounts of this incident, readily available online.

exactly what that is, even if they couldn't articulate their dominance as *privilege*. But they knew they were dominant. They could stand face-to-face and stare down anyone. Or at least that's what they wanted you to believe.

They had no problem staring me down. I was one of their most likely and available targets.

To be bullied is to be subjected to prolonged harassment, day in, day out, a steady regime of terror and torment. The ceaseless taunting and verbal abuse became the thousand paper cuts that nearly bled me dry, that tore into my psyche in ways that will be with me until I die. Faggot, queer, pussy, fag, fudge-packer, cocksucker: these were the taunts of choice for teen boys in the 1980s. I don't ever recall — not once — a teacher hearing such verbal abuse and calling it out, chastising a student, marking their name-calling as wrong. Back then, in the late '70s and early '80s, it wasn't understood as abuse. It was just what boys did. Some teachers probably believed that such taunting would toughen me up. I was a bit shy, even aloof, soft. *Easily penetrable.* I needed to be harder. Verbal assault would help, or so they thought. I would "man up." Perhaps I'd even fight back. Be a man, not a pussy.

Don't be a pussy. That is, don't be the penetrable male. Don't let us rape you. Real men stand up for themselves. They don't let themselves be penetrated.

But I didn't know how. I knew deep in my heart that I really was, very likely, a faggot, queer, pussy, fag, fudge-packer, cocksucker. I was being called out. I was being interpellated. Hail, faggot. Yeah, you. You're looking this way when I called so you *must* be a faggot.

A male friend my age, asked me later in mid-life if it had been that bad. After all, weren't most of us in the '80s called such names? Even he, a straight man, was called faggot at times. You lived with it, he said. You tossed it back.

No, it's not the same, my dear straight friend, my age mate, you weren't really grappling with your sexuality in quite the same way. You didn't identify with the term "faggot" because you were already enjoying the comfortable privilege of normalcy. The insult wasn't aimed at you, not really, or if it was, it was a misfire. Indeed, the taunt likely straightened you out even further. It stiffened your back, squared your shoulders a bit. But that's the point; you didn't bow, you didn't bend beneath it, flinch under it.

I did.

The psychic damage of being called out — every single day, every single fucking day — by terms of not just derision but *hatred,* terms that identify the desires that you're grappling with, the very sensibilities and proclivities that interest you and, in fact, actually draw your interest to other boys — when those desires and proclivities are, on a daily basis, treated with scorn and contempt and *hatred,* then you are damaged *on a daily basis,* the damage accumulating over time, over years, becoming self-hatred, internalized shame, interpolated rage. How could I not grow up to hate myself when I was so constantly told, so ceaselessly reminded, that I was *to be hated.* And when no adult around you stops it, when in fact the message is clear: you deserve this — then how could I not feel that my self-hatred was justified, when the hatred of others was confirmed by the absence of a restraining hand, a merciful reprieve?

A hole opened up in me, and these boys, these catholic schoolboys, fucked it every day, over and over again, sometimes slowly, lingeringly, often quickly, jabbing — fag, fag, fag, fag, fag.

***

One of the most harrowing experiences I had as a teenager was actually not on the campus of my high school but on the phone. Boys would call my parents' house, prank calling frequently, sometimes hurling taunts before hanging up. Remember that this is before the time of caller ID. We couldn't know who these boys were, who was calling, but they were so obviously from my high school, which made available phone numbers of all students in some misguided attempt to cultivate community. Instead, it cultivated abuse.

A boy called up one afternoon and actually stayed on the line for a good long time, *Faggot, you're a motherfucking faggot. We're going to beat your ass. We're going to send your faggot ass to the hospital. Your mother won't be able to buy groceries because your hospital bills are going to be so high. Fucking faggot. You deserve to die.*

I note that he stayed on the line for a good long time. I guess I did too. I didn't hang up. What battle was I choosing in that moment? What fight did I think I could win? Or did I feel that, by this point, I just deserved this abuse? Perhaps I needed to hear this, even wanted to hear this, confirming my worst fears about myself. I deserved to die.

Or was something else happening here, something else operating? Fear turned to freeze? Even today, I feel stunned by the specificity of the threat: *your mother won't be able to buy groceries.* I come back again and again to this threat — your mother won't be able to buy groceries — because it is so particular, so pointed, even so oddly poignant in the horror that it attempts to deliver. I wonder, I have to wonder: What was going through this boy's mind? How did he remotely think that it was OK not just to threaten someone's life, to state explicitly that he and his compatriots wanted to inflict bodily harm, but then to go the extra-added step to imagine a domestic scene, to picture my mother, overwhelmed with the mounting hospital bills from their assault on my body, unable to buy food for her family?

I try to imagine what they must've been imagining, what they depicted to themselves as they— for surely it's a "they," a collective of hatred that scripted this phone call — sought to deliver the maximum sense of fear. One would think that, once they got to the mother in this, once they might have imagined their own mothers reacting to such a threat, that they would've pulled back. *We're going too far, it's just too much. Yeah, let's tease the faggot, but leave the mother out of it.* But no. They didn't hold back. They stood their ground like the MAGA-capped boys. And then proceeded further.

I do not know what the boy on the phone was thinking or imagining or feeling. Maybe I don't really want to know. I've never felt that I could call someone else up and threaten them in such a way. I don't think of myself as a particularly good person, and I've certainly been angry and hurt and have wished others ill. But I don't believe I've consciously or intentionally visited horror on someone else.

And now, nearly every day I imagine that horror visited on me. I wake up in the middle of the night, test the security of our front door, going back again to test the knob, make sure it's locked, then pull again on the door, ensure that it's safe, that we are safe, that my husband and I are safe, that my mother who now lives with us in her elderly years is safe. I imagine them coming for us. I imagine them on the other side of the door, wanting in, wanting to kill us, wanting first to torture us. *Fucking faggots. Motherfucking faggots. And the mother, the fucking mother who birthed this faggot. Die, faggots. You deserve to die.* I test the security of the door. It's locked, for now. It's OK. We're going to be OK. I try to go back to sleep.

***

What are the ways in which we come to accept abuse? And what are the ways in which the larger culture, the larger politics, positions us to accept — perhaps expect — abuse?

Here's where it gets hard, as though it wasn't already.

I've always had an attraction to bullies, to the boys who would push around and make fun of other boys, who were just a bit bigger and more badass than we were, than I was. A *lot* more than I was. I'm not always sure that I wanted to be *like* them, and I was never under the impression that they would like me. This is something that lies slightly outside some of the formulas I know about attraction and desire. Jonathan Dollimore, in *Sexual Dissidence,* a book I kept close to me as a young adult for it seemed to explain so much, tried to queerly muddy the waters a bit between the various formulations of desire authorized and approved by our heteropatriarchal culture. On one hand, as Dollimore theorizes, with members of the opposite sex, you could safely say, "I like you." But with members of the *same* sex, you were supposed to say, "I want to *be like* you." Dollimore smartly understood the two injunctions as potentially slipping into and out of one another, so that a boy admiring another boy and wanting to be like him could at times feel that his desire to be like the other boy might actually be his *liking* of the other boy. Of course, this was the danger to be acutely avoided. Embracing your queerness means you don't avoid the danger; you relish it.

As intellectually profound and stimulating as I found this analysis in the 1990s, it didn't help me understand my (admittedly and self-diagnosedly perverse) fascination with bullies. I didn't want to be like them, and I frankly didn't even *like* them very much at all. But I did want to control them, or at least manage their hostility toward me. So befriending, or at least trying to befriend them, often seemed a good strategy. If they'd only like me just a little bit, perhaps they wouldn't want to hurt me.

So I'd befriend the bully, or at least try to. I'd offer to help out with homework, do the problems that they couldn't, solve the equations they stumbled upon, perform the analyses that eluded them. I was pathetic. I'd even imagine at night their arms encircling me in a gesture of protection. That never happened.

Except for one boy, who taunted me for most of a summer — in our church, yes, in our church youth group, with no adults pulling this little fucker aside to chastise him for being a dick. All summer long, out of the earshot of adults, but sometimes with them surreptitiously listening in, I was faggot this, faggot that, queer, "that way." He was loud, rude, obnoxious. All the other kids looked up to him. Just visiting for one summer, he rolled in to transform our little youth group into his posse, and I was most definitely the queer one, the one tolerated just because I could be made fun of. This boy approached me just days before he was to return home to Georgia, put his hand over my mouth, and forcefully kissed his hand. "That's what you want, isn't it?" I didn't respond, couldn't, because I'd been called out. And while I don't recall ever having had any kind of overtly sexual attraction to this young punk, I did feel somewhat nostalgic upon his departure. I felt I would actually miss him. I would miss my bully.

Everyone in church that year was singing Michael W. Smith's pop gospel hit "Friends." I was learning to play the song on the piano, and I'd sit alone and play it, thinking of this boy:

> Packing up the dreams God planted
> In the fertile soil of you
> Can't believe the hopes He's granted
> Means a chapter in your life is through
> But we'll keep you close as always
> It won't even seem you've gone
> 'Cause our hearts in big and small ways
> Will keep the love that keeps us strong[3]

I can't help but think that a normal young man would've been ecstatic to see this little shit go home. But I felt keenly the loss of a chapter in our shared life, the story of the tormenter and the

---

[3]   "Friends" by Michael W. Smith, here performed live: https://www.youtube.com/watch?v=SAeD2UEYaAk. Smith released a pop album in 1990 called *Go West Young Man,* which I listened to repeatedly along with Annie Lennox's *Diva* in 1992. I was clearly... caught between worlds? finding solace as I could? wondering what the hell was I doing?

tormented — his parting kiss a perversely queer recognition of the intimate bond between us.

I haven't thought of this kid in years, but in retrospect he seems so typical of the kind of bully that I would attempt to befriend. I would at times try to tolerate the insults. I would try to engage him in conversation. I'd express an interest in his interests, football, always football with these Southern boys, a sport I loathed. But I knew that my primary value lay in my ability to be abused, to withstand the abuse, to keep coming back for more. "That's what you want, isn't it?" If they'd only like me just a little bit, I thought, perhaps they wouldn't want to hurt me.

I have to write that sentence again, because I recognize how — Dollimore-like — the sentence wants to slip into its shadow desire, its intimate corollary: *If they'd only like me just a little bit, perhaps I can tell them better how to hurt me.*

***

As I'm writing this, I'm sitting across from the group of young men who come to this coffeeshop every Tuesday to pray. Protestants call this fellowship, although these boys, all in their twenties, could be catholics. I suspect not, though, because I've rarely seen catholics occupy a space like this so assertively; catholics have their own spaces, built on millennia of wealth-building.

These boys visit, talk about their lives, bullshit one another, and then bow their heads to pray before parting with bumped fists and affirmations to have a blessed week. I find them both frightening and tantalizing. They're all good-looking, perhaps their good looks augmented by earnestness; after all, you have to be pretty earnest or want at least to affect some earnestness if you're going to pray in public. I'm looking at one in particular, his head bowed, shoulders slumped over, his khaki-clad butt projecting just every so enticingly over the bench on which he sits. Their god likely does not want me checking out this kid's rear end, and perhaps that also contributes to the attraction — an attraction I've learned to indulge despite the fear I was taught about such desires.

And it is here, in the cultivation of this fear in me, that all of these christians come together in my mind, whether they are catholic, protestant, mormon, or whatnot. I associate them with fear, with the willful granting of fear like droplets of grace they bestow on those around them who are not wanted, who are to be despised, the wicked and wretched of the earth, those destined for the places of darkness and suffering, their earthly torment only a foretaste of what is to come in the afterlife, the realm of weeping and gnashing of teeth.

I look below the khaki-clad ass and see their variously sneakered feet, multiple pairs under the wooden bench they share, many of these feet tapping, keeping time to their words, but some of them tapping tapping with nervousness. Do some of these boys feel the fear too? Or is this just nerves from praying in public, something a bit edgy in this hipster cafe? I don't know, and I won't ask. But I can wonder. I do wonder. I wonder about these people far too frequently. What propels them to give fear so freely to those not like them, who do not believe like them, who otherwise preach the gospel of love?

* * *

As I was finishing up my graduate studies and about to be married, I worried that my feelings for men would complicate my marriage. Writing that now seems so strange, and I suspect that it will strike some of you as strange as well, especially if you've grown up in a queerer time and place, where the possibilities for imagining a queer life are more abundant, or at least not as severely constrained as they were in my time and place. But no, for much of my youth, I couldn't imagine a queer life. No one around me was really living much of a queer life. Given that this was the Deep South in the '80s, Reagan's '80s, no one in my usual spheres was openly gay. Not after my uncle died. He had been the only one. And he died, horribly, of cancer.

And then, in my early twenties, I started working in a restaurant. During the summers, my girlfriend, studying at Boston College, would head back to the New Orleans area and work at a chain Mexican restaurant, so one summer I decided to join her, making some extra cash. Here's where I met some of my first openly gay people my age. Well, as I recall, I think it was actually just two openly gay people. Maybe three. I equivocate, because there were probably no more than two at a time, although rampant speculation about one or two other employees ran wild. We were mostly young, a bit high-strung, some lives more precarious than others. My girlfriend and I probably felt more secure than many others, who actually depended on the income of the place to make ends meet. We were still in school, so the work was more for spending cash than anything else. Perhaps the precarity — and the time and place — combined to keep a few folks deeper in the closet. But not everyone.

One young man was particularly flaming, as we used to say. In fact, he was flamboyant enough, swaying his hips to the piped in music while waiting for his food to come up in the window, snapping his fingers and catcalling the cuter guys, so open and seemingly at ease in his petit dancer's body, that my girlfriend and I called him, just to ourselves, "fag world." I blush to recall this. But we did. And I know that we actually liked this young man. It was hard *not* to like him. He seemed always possessed of such good cheer, always ready to drift into song as he talked, as though his life were just about to become a piece of extravagant musical theater. He was fun to be around. We even went out drinking a few times with him, or out to eat after our shifts ended, or, just a couple times, out dancing in a local club. His being so out and proud, as we would say now, didn't seem to bother anyone, at least not that I could recall. And even when we spoke about him privately, commenting on what outrageous thing "fag world" had done this time, or what sketchy thing he'd said, we didn't say "fag" to one another with contempt. It was more a marker, a differentiation, a noting that his world was not our world. Of course, even in the Deep South, we knew better than to say it to his face; it wasn't a friendly thing to say at all. Not everyone knew better, though, and he certainly got his share of homophobic comments and hostile looks — all of which he'd laugh off, spritely skipping away before the interaction could get too serious. The customer is always right, after all.

I remember this young man and think to myself — could I have followed him to some different world? Surely he represented a door in the wall, some chink in the armor of the homophobic and heteronormative world that I had grown up in. I think that I might have come close one evening. My girlfriend had gone back to Boston to take a summer class, and, as was not at all unusual at the end of a shift, a few of us talked about heading out for a drink, some late dinner. We did, and then this young man, fag world, wanted to go dancing. No one else did, but I decided that I'd go with him. He was quite good. And while we didn't dance together, I enjoyed watching him cut up the dance floor. Actually, you couldn't really dance *with* him; he was far too much of a performer. But it was still fun. There was no erotic energy between us at all, no erotic energy, but perhaps an unspoken invitation. A set of gestures, smiles, and subtle winks that offered to accompany me somewhere else. I sat calmly with my drink, watching him dance, knowing that I would be married the following summer.

I want to be honest about my life and recognize the moments when I might have chosen a different path. But I also want to be honest about some of the impossibilities of choice. For in that moment, watching this young gay man dance, watching fag world dance, I was offered a choice that I could not choose. Not that I wouldn't, or didn't, but that I *could not choose*. There was nothing in my life — not family, not church, not the lion's share of my friends, not all of the past I had experienced, not all of the discourses of sexism and homophobia that had surrounded me since birth — there was not anything in my life that would have made following this young man out of that dance club seem like a remotely viable option. I knew that world existed. I remembered my uncle and his partner. I knew there was a door, however small, but still a door in the wall. And my response was to say no, fag world, I cannot follow you. It was the only response I had to offer.

I want you to understand, and I'm going to fail to communicate this to you, that there are choices that are not choices. There are opportunities that signal only that you cannot accept them. There are possibilities that only tease and that you turn away from with melancholy, with sad smiles, with missed chances that you then, later in life, tell yourself weren't really chances at all because, in the moment of the chance, in the offer of the key to the door in the wall, there's nothing in your life that has prepared you to take that key, to take that chance.

My only response to this young man could be, sadly, to mark him and his life as "fag world," behind his back, a little shamefully, knowing my own curiosity, but turning away because I was convinced that this was not the path for me. Turning away because I had been convinced (passive voice) that this was not the path for me. Turning away because I had been convinced that his was the path of AIDS, abuse, violation, death. None of his extravagant dancing, such masterful swaying of hips and bon vivant spirit, none of that could convince me otherwise, could convince me that his path went anywhere other than to misery and despair, a mother crying, a mother not able to buy groceries for her children.

***

Getting closer to my wedding, I was desperate enough not to be gay that I sought out psychotherapy. No, not reparative therapy. Reparative therapy would have required that I actively acknowledge that I thought about young men, that I had intense feelings for men of a distinctly erotic nature, that I was *interested* in men. That I was not prepared to do. I'm not entirely certain that I could have acknowledged such interests to myself—but that current uncertainty stems perhaps from a sense that, surely, if I had those feelings, if I beat off to the thought of other young men, then surely I was approaching, had very likely already approached, the possibility of articulating that I was gay. Is that not totally likely? Even asking the question now seems absurd; of course, it was likely. And yet I didn't. I was probably twenty-six or twenty-seven before I announced that I was bisexual.

But wait. This isn't true. This can't possibly be true. *What is truth here?* I can only tally up the possible truths. I've tried to write about this before. Was I not successful? Have I not already arrived at the truth? Writing this now, I find myself sitting up straighter, tucking my tail bone in. This is a test. This is always a test. *What is the truth here?*

I first masturbated—but wait—I must say that I first masturbated *unknowingly* in that I wasn't aware that I was masturbating, so it's more correct, I suppose, to say that I had my first completely unintended orgasm after I'd tied myself up and lay writhing on the carpet of my bedroom. I imagined myself a captured superhero. I probably had a pair of tighty whities slipped over my khaki schoolboy pants, my bounds formed from my sister's jump rope. Jesus, all the fucking strange collisions and intertwinings of erotic possibility here, manifesting in future decades of sexual twists and turns: underwear, cartoons, bondage, filial connections and drama…. I digress. Point here: I wasn't thinking of a boy in particular but perhaps boyhood in general. Writhing boyhood. Being captured. Enjoying the torment of capture. But also the captured *superhero*, the latent power, the promise of power. I was strong, even if others didn't know it.

Next: playing tie-up games with my friends, always switching back and forth between putting them in bondage and letting them put me in bondage, and then advancing later in my adolescence to absurd penalty games with my friends as we played RISK, the board game of world conquest, with the losers inevitably experiencing some kind of restraint or torture. I was always a little surprised at the readiness of so many friends, even in high school to engage in these perverse little games. But just for fun. Just a bet. Nothing sexually, hardly.

Next: continuing the tie-up games through early adulthood but alone, tying myself up to get off. When I masturbated, I thought of women tying me up but also got off thinking of me tying up men. This seemed a butch enough reconciliation. Totally OK to think of men while masturbating if I was dominating them. That somehow reinforced my sense of my own masculinity. I was powerful.

Next: starting to date young women, but never having sex with them, claiming that my christianity prevented me from doing that, saving myself for the right one, but talking one of them into tying me up upon occasion. I remember one time in particular, for my nineteenth birthday, the young woman, perhaps a couple of years older than me, already sexually experienced, perhaps a bit frustrated by my unwillingness to go all the way, tying me up to the bed, my hands bound above my head to a post of some kind. We writhe on the bed, me ducking her attempts to give me a hickey. We're both still fully clothed. Our gymnastics escalate and a glass of vodka and orange juice, a homemade screwdriver, topples off the nightstand. She rushes to get a towel, while I tell her that I should be disciplined for this. She flips me over and whips my ass. Minutes later I'm creaming my shorts, but I don't tell her I've had an orgasm, my first in the presence of another human being.

Next: just before I'm married, my wife ties me up and I have an orgasm. Of course we will have sex during our marriage. I will enjoy it. Even when I have sex once while she's on her period, my cock coming out of her covered in blood, I didn't mind really. It wasn't disgusting to me. She didn't intend it to happen. But I really didn't mind.

But wait: I'm skipping something. That last year of my under-graduate days in college. Fuck. I've already written about this. I'll try to telegraph it here. It's not enough. It won't be enough. But I can't not say it. There were moments — and note how everything here at the sentence level slips into a deferral of agency: "it's not," "there were" — there were moments when I'd talk friends into going to the gay bar down the street. Nothing ever happened. If I was cruised (again the passive, because I'm not doing the cruising, because I didn't even know how to cruise, because I didn't even know what the word "cruise" meant) — if I was cruised, I wouldn't have known. Except one time: this very large man followed me around the bar, trying to catch my attention. Older man, but not old. Probably a nice guy. I fled every time. My friends probably thought I was struggling with my sexuality but they rarely mentioned this, except for a little joking: *Oh you, wanting to go to the gay bar, what's up with that? But let's go; it'll be fun; something different. Something edgy.*

And then, wait for it: the moment during my senior year, on my own, no girlfriend, falling in love with a straight boy, a story I won't rehearse here at any length, it's just too sad (again the deferral: it's too sad). But yes, actually — and yes, I admit it, I know it, I cannot deny, not now and not then, certainly not — I know I'm in love, I know this is a crush, it's nothing but a crush, but of course it's everything because it was crushing me. And this boy wanted nothing to do with me. Friend of friends, so I'd see him sometimes in our various circles, but he wanted nothing to do with me. It was crushing. I imagined tying him to my bed, face down, shaving his ass, and violating him with something, like a large firm vegetable. Humiliating him. Transferring my humiliation to him. But him also somehow delighting in this, a masochist after all. It's all projection here.

And then, speaking of projection, I, a senior in college, pro-posed a film series at the student union, "Homosexuality in Film," which didn't make it, but I knew what I was doing. My friend group at the time, so different than my previous friends, now young people like me wondering about themselves, willing to experiment. The freedom of college, the experimentation. We self-consciously called ourselves, at least some of us, the "New Decadence," trying on this term, "decadence," not sure if we really meant it. And then ironically, or so we thought, ironically, would have "heterosexual nights out," pairing up boy and girl to play at being straight, because some of us at least knew that, deep down, we were so queer, so very queer, although none of us were using that word at the time. Remember: 1980s. Reagan's America. We still very much imagined nuclear devastation as the end of our lives. Or nuclear family. We're only experimenting after all.

But then, but then — what is it? What is *it*? It was, when I was 21, about to graduate, finally kissing a boy, full on the mouth, one drunken night, one very drunken night, the group of us in my dorm room, drinking, talking, dog-piling, boys and girls together, the group of us fondling one another, but pulling back from actual sex, just experimenting. And then I kissed a boy, thinking right away, how odd to feel his stubble, I'd never felt stubble before. And I'm writing this right now, in this coffee-shop on an early winter morning, and tears are coming to my eyes, remembering this, remembering this, feeling his stubble, so very odd to feel his stubble, it's not quite right, I've never felt stubble when kissing someone before, but I keep kissing, I want to feel the stubble, knowing that I will want to feel the stubble again, if not with this boy, with some boy, feeling the stubble. I know this.

Next: it's all over soon enough. It? Yes, it, all of it. Let me tell you. We were drinking pretty heavily that term. I was definitely drinking pretty heavily that term. Some of us were about to graduate — a scary prospect generally, but scary I think also for me in that I knew but couldn't acknowledge, knew in the gut, in the marrow of the bone, in the small animal part of the brain that lashes out when cornered, that I would have to make a decision about being gay or not, about kissing another boy with stubble. But like I said: I couldn't articulate that to myself, even though, in retrospect, writing from some distance, it seems like the only question I could have been grappling with.

Again, *it,* again, with the *it.* The it that is placed backward in time, that is cast from what I know now into a past that I didn't know I was writing at the time. It's a truism, a truth generally received but not always understood: we see ourselves through the ways of seeing we have become accustomed to seeing, and that goes for our past selves as well. No recollection in tranquility, not remembrance of things past. We violate the past with what we know now. I'm screaming at that kid: *what the fuck, what the fucking fuck,* but those screams are from the part of me that wants now all of that time back, all of that blasted time back, and wishes that that boy had had an opportunity to become the gay man that he wanted to be in his bones but couldn't bring himself to grow into. Even now, the violence I'm doing to my younger self is placing, more like burying, an identity into him, an identity within a possibility, deep in his bones, where he couldn't even begin to think that being gay was a possibility, much less an identity. Because for him it wasn't a possibility. It was only experimenting. Just playing. There were no survivable scripts that had him starring as a gay hero. There was nothing but AIDS and social ostracism and family shame and the sulphur-fueled fires of eternity. He could kiss a boy with stubble, he could drunkenly kiss a boy with stubble, but this kiss is only ever a mistake, a thrilling experiment, and also the path one knows one shouldn't take, the scattering of seeds on infertile soil. He believes this, he knows this, even if the knowledges of the body are saying this mistake, this experiment, is good. But it's not. This boy will numb his feelings with alcohol, will try to drown what he's doing with so much alcohol that I'm only grateful as the man-child of this boy that he didn't really hurt himself, that he didn't drive headlong into an oncoming car as he very well could have, driving one night with a friend, unable to see the road clearly, focusing on one dashed white line after another, one white line, another, and another, just to stay on the road. His friends see him as damaged, dangerous. They drift away. They claim not to know him, not to really know him. The stubble boy leaves, ill equipped himself to deal with this much self-hatred because he has enough of his own shit to contend with, being gay in the

Deep South, in the deepest of souths. The boy, me this time, me, I am writing a thesis on the poetry of the First World War, Wilfred Owen, another boy-lover, but all I see is Owen dying in the war, at the end of the war, just days before it's over, before it's all over, he dies, he gets what he deserves, a life spent yearning for the boys in his military care and his just reward is death before he can go home and enjoy having survived. He doesn't survive. *You won't survive this.* I knew I wouldn't survive this.

No one survives this. The great lie. No one survives this.

The problem was that I was sinning, a sinner in the hands of an angry god, a god who was not just twitching on the thread but yanking my ass back in line, who had had enough, who had fucking had enough, *this shit has got to stop, you are destroying yourself, my creation, my beautiful boy.* I want to hold this boy. I want to touch this young man. I want to lie down again with him in his bed, late at night, a pathetic lamp on a pathetic milk crate illuminating the book he's reading, yet another book he's reading from the library as he looks for books about himself, about other boys like himself, and so many of them, still so many of them, about boys like him who are dying. And then he finds one, William Maxwell's *The Folded Leaf,* two boys, two boys together clinging, two boys at a boarding school, earlier in the century, having to sleep in the same bed because that's how boys at that time kept warm in the dead of winter, and there's no sex, not a hint of sex, nothing sexual, there's nothing sexual here, and one boy loves the other boy, and the other boy loves the first boy, and late at night, huddled back to back against the cold, one boy falls asleep first and the other boy lies awake thinking, thinking, thinking and feeling, but it's all good, it's all pure, and he moves his foot, curling his toes into the arched back of the other boy's foot, and with this simple pure movement he launches himself into dreams that he will not remember. This is what I remember of that passage, concluding a chapter, one boy curling his foot into another and then going to sleep. This is the most I could've dreamed for, this is the most I still dream for, this is the most that I have ever wanted, this is what I was able to understand, in that moment, in that place, reading all of these books about other boys dying because they loved too much, they loved too wrongly, seeing boys and men and old men dying on the television because they have loved *wrongly* — this is the most I can hope for: one boy, another boy, one boy curling his toes into the foot of another. And then sleep. Sleep with dreams you will not remember because they are too much, too much. The truth is too much.

But what is the truth here? The truth is that I tried. I experimented. I dabbled. I put my foot in the queer water. But I couldn't overcome everything that I thought I knew about being gay — and that, ultimately, with all of these feelings, I believed of myself that *I am too much.* I will be told, I have been told, I was always told, *you are too much, too much, all of this is just too much.*

* * *

So many memories, memories of things I might have done, but also of reading, looking, searching, trying to find the others, any others, like me, possibly like me. I glimpsed them in *The Folded Leaf*. Where else might they have been? Where else, who else? Tricky here, always tricky. Be careful what you ask for, what you might find.

I'm remembering Evelyn Waugh, not that I knew him, but I certainly knew his work, which is strange because he's such a precious writer, a British satirist. I'm only now realizing the influence his work had on my life, how it reaffirmed in so many ways the homophobic world built around me. I encountered him first through the televised version of *Brideshead Revisited* in the 1980s, that lushly beautiful and languorously indulgent production with a star-studded cast, including small roles by the likes of John Gielgud and Laurence Olivier, but the major roles, the two boys, played by a very young Jeremy Irons and Anthony Andrews. If you don't know the series, the book, or even the rather not good movie version from 2008, you're missing out, something I can still say. Don't get me wrong: this book fucked me up, or if it itself didn't exactly fuck me up, it was most definitely part of the problem.[4]

Brideshead Revisited, subtitled the "sacred and profane memories of Captain Charles Ryder," is about a middle-aged army captain during the height of the Second World War, stumbling with his unit through England and coming across an old, largely abandoned manor — the scene of his dense entanglement with a rich family, the Flytes. The sight of the house propels him into memory and reassessment, compelling him to reexamine the botched course of his life to this point — and, by extension in Waugh's mind, I believe — the botched course of European history that has plunged the world into yet another global conflict. But what captivates a reader and then a viewer of the miniseries, well over and beyond Waugh's drift to moralizing, is the relationship between Ryder, solidly of the middle class, and the

---

4 *The Folded Leaf* and *Brideshead Revisited* were apparently both originally published in 1945.

decadent aristocratic Flytes, two of whom he falls in love with, although one might argue that he's fallen in love with the entire family. It's hard love, tough. The Flytes are part of a dying breed, and you get the sense that Waugh, himself the socialite, bemoans a little bit the passing of the landed gentry, the rich overlords, the keeper of the flame of British greatness, blah blah blah. I wasn't watching the series or reading the book at fifteen and sixteen and thinking about the British landed gentry, though I admit that I loved the luxuriousness of the sets, the scenes, even the music, whose theme song I hummed to myself as I watched the series in my lower middle-class parents' home in the greater New Orleans suburbs.

What drew me in to such a rarefied world? I wanted a family, like Charles did, to broaden my world, to expand my horizons, to take me up and envelop me in some other drama that wasn't my own, my family's, the limited and stifling realm of the catholic schools that bounded my world. Even more temptingly, Charles is an artist, a character with whom I could all too easily identify and imagine myself, like him, misunderstood by his own distant father and eagerly looking for something else, something more, something beyond. The Flytes, and the series and book by extension, provided me access to that other, that beyond — at least at first.

What was this gateway to this other world, this expanded sense of the possible? Surely the early scenes of Charles and Sebastian, meeting at Oxford as Sebastian, stumbling home one night from a bender, leans through a window of Charles's room and vomits profusely. Sebastian invites Charles to a make-up lunch, and not only is all forgiven but a life-changing friendship develops. The two are inseparable, Charles spending more and more time with the Flytes at Brideshead. Of course, Waugh wants you to wonder what exactly the Flytes are in flight from, what are they trying to escape, what past, what responsibility, what stiff-upper lip duty demands such evacuation that some of them would rather set themselves on a course of self-destruction than own up to their inherited moral imperative. They're catholics, as Waugh was, but lapsed. Sebastian is, fetchingly, the worst of the lot—a beauty but clearly an alcoholic, charming but very likely toxic. His and Charles's friendship, and its twists and turns, dominates the first half of the book before Charles eventually marries Sebastian's sister, Julia. The story of their unsuccessful marriage—homoerotic displacement?—occupies the book's latter half. Charles, Julia, and other characters steadily grope their way toward some kind of recognition that God won't let them go, that they cannot help but believe in Him, etc. I say "etc." here because none of it seems completely convincing. Waugh was better as a satirist, even if a catholic moralizing animated that satire, that snarky, snarling critique of a society that he felt was foolish, shallow, and foppish.

But Waugh liked his fops. They're everywhere in his fiction. And if he doesn't ultimately side with them, he certainly fell enough in love with them that they remain some of his most interesting characters. Sebastian for one, but also Anthony Blanche, the *obvious* homosexual aesthete in *Brideshead* who lures, tempts, seduces the boys into underground gay bars, prodigious drinking, and god knows what else isn't scripted into the pages of the book. Anthony Blanche is a stereotype, flamboyant and effeminate, but he was one of the very first openly gay characters I ever saw on television and then ever read about in a work of literature. I was enraptured. I couldn't *not* watch him, keeping vigil for his all-too-rare appearances in the miniseries.

The next best thing in the show and the book for me was the tender scenes between Charles and Sebastian, their developing friendship and intimacy, their easy camaraderie, the way they leaned into one another on a gondola in Venice, the way they sunbathed nude. Irons's and Andrews's taut naked buttocks might have been my very first porn. But it was also the intimacy of their relationship that captured me—the friend, the best friend, the only friend. The one. Sebastian's dissolute father (played by Laurence Olivier!) had a mistress who spotted this special friendship, remarking on it, even acknowledging that it's a good thing and that the father's lack of it in his own youth has very likely fucked him up, robbing him of the chance to practice the codes and protocols of intimacy with a friend. But it's only supposed to be *practice*. Such friendship is doomed if it goes on too long. It must be replaced in time with proper marriage, heterosexual marriage, by Charles's love for Julia.

Of course it must, as this is a catholic novel written by a catholic author, who, like most satirists deep down is a moralist — and this one with a pre-scripted code of conduct. But still... and still... Waugh risked these portrayals — Anthony Blanche, and the friendship between Sebastian and Charles, which is never confirmed as a sexual one but clearly marked as intimate, a great love, a first love. Waugh can't help but punish Sebastian, ultimately. He flees his family (and perhaps Charles?) to northern Africa, taking up with a noxious (if cute) German, and dying of alcoholism, Charles at his bedside, a warning to Charles, a lesson needing learning.

The lesson wasn't lost on me. You could have this great friendship, but if you persisted, if it lasted too long, this was the end. Death was the end of this. Your death. You wouldn't survive the ongoingness of this immature love, this practice intimacy, this childhood crush, this childish thing that must be put away. *Brideshead Revisited* aired as a miniseries in 1981, I was watching it in 1983, and I had read the book by 1984 — just in time for the specter of AIDS, the dying face of Rock Hudson in 1985, to confirm the lessons of the elder catholic Waugh, the lessons surrounding me in my catholic school, my baptist church, my rural-raised parents.

And yet... and yet. While I know that this book, while I know now, looking back, that this book was part of the problem, I want to hold on to it. I want to read it badly, as I read it badly at the time, latching on to the dirty parts, the evil parts, the degenerate characters — because they spoke to me. I want to hold on to this book even now, thinking that Waugh understood the pleasures and possibilities of queerness even if he couldn't enjoy the pleasures and possibilities himself. After all, it's Anthony Blanche who warns Charles about the Flytes, about how shallow they are, about their dangerous charm. He criticizes Charles's art at an exhibit, bemoaning how enraptured, how captivated, how trapped Charles has been by this family:

I was right years ago — more years, I am happy to say, than either of us shows — when I warned you. I took you out to dinner to warn you of charm. I warned you expressly and in great detail of the Flyte family. Charm is the great English blight. It does not exist outside these damp islands. It spots and kills anything it touches. It kills love; it kills art; I greatly fear, my dear Charles, it has killed you.

We can read this critique, this warning, as the devil quoting scripture, as Waugh putting in the words of his most debauched character the truths that he most wanted to believe in: that allowing yourself to be charmed into flight from your duty, your responsibility, your moral obligations will ultimately corrupt everything about you, even the gifts and talents that God gave you. Fair enough, Evelyn, fair enough. But I also want to read this as a calling to Charles not to accept secondhand goods, not to be flattered and entranced by the appearance of the degenerate, the fake evil of the Flytes who only pretend to be evil, who viciously hate themselves for turning away from their God to the sins of the flesh, who must purge their corruption by drinking themselves to death.

I hear Anthony saying, no, if you're going to go bad, go *all the way bad*. Don't be charmed. Don't settle for appearances. Don't just *play* at the bad. I warn you expressly and in great detail: embrace your wickedness.

* * *

I wasn't ready to hear that advice, put quite that way, articulated so expressly. Instead, I turned to a counselor, still in my early twenties, wanting to flee myself. Counselor. Hmm, I wonder. I don't remember his name, I don't remember what he looked like. White male, probably late thirtyish? Typical straight guy, with not much disrespect meant when I say that. Christian. That I remember. My fiancée and I had been going to Campus Crusade for Christ meetings, which I recall as somewhat rowdy prayer groups. Generally innocuous, not overly fundamentalist or even evangelical as I recall. *Not* innocuous in the sense that *none* of such groups can be truly innocuous, their goal, ultimately, to persuade you to follow a particular path of salvation or reinforce your sense of the world along their lines. Religions rely on indoctrination, and then further inoculation against belief systems that might deter you from the path, the straight and narrow path that aligns your thoughts, feelings, and body in accordance with prescribed beliefs.

So no, not innocuous, this particular Campus Crusade (Crusade! The War is on!), but perhaps not overly assaulting. Some singing, some prayer, some positive affirmations and exhortations to carry Christ with you in all things. How seemingly different from the catholicism of *Brideshead Revisited,* which seems like just so much aesthetic background — visits to a quaint chapel on the manor grounds, chats with a priest in his silky robes, an arty staging that you discover too late has seeped into your soul: you *must* believe, God twitching on your thread, pulling you back in line, one of the faithful after all. You bury your head in Father's robes, relieved, even glad. In its own way, Campus Crusade for Christ operated under a similar paradigm albeit with very different protocols. Far less aesthetically lush, the music was nonetheless meant to be affectively stirring —

Our God is an awesome God he reigns
From heaven above with wisdom, power and love
Our God is an awesome God[5]

---

5   "Our God Is an Awesome God" was written by Michael W. Smith.

— designed to be sung communally, the words and tunes reinforcing one another, the pop-rock drumbeats finding resonance in the vibrations of your soul, bringing you into sonic and somatic alignment with the message: Our God is awesome; he reigns, he is powerful. (Crusade!)

So, of course, I would turn to him to help me, the counselor representing God, representing too the father who was always distant from me, who likely never really loved me. I would find God and father at last (at least?) in this counselor. Ok, not really. I was twenty-five and I understood some of the rudiments of transference. I was old enough not to need to be cuddled by an actual male parent, and I knew that the counselor wouldn't cuddle me. But I hoped he would help me. I believed he could help me.

He was nice enough, that I remember. And while I can't recall him at all much physically, I do recall the gentle brown surroundings of his office, the soft couch on which I sat, the books and knickknacks surrounding us, speaking of smart comfort, knowledgeable ease, no pressure, just talking, talking. Crying is OK. I don't think I cried. I'm pretty sure I never cried in any therapist's office. I saw this man just a handful of times, maybe four or five. He recommended some books to read after I talked about how I think my uncle had molested me as a child and that I worried that I wouldn't be man enough for my wife, I wouldn't be able to satisfy her. I so wanted to be a good husband, but I had concerns, I had issues, I was afraid that I had lost my path on the straight and narrow, the true course of my development had somehow been derailed — no, not somehow, had very probably been derailed by my uncle fondling me as a child. No, I had no specifics, I could recall no details, and the counselor wasn't asking for them, nothing salacious required here, nothing untoward, no need to relive this trauma, even and perhaps especially if you can't quite recall it. *It's all going to be OK, God can take care of this, God can handle this, give this to God. He can bear you up on eagle's wings* — oh wait: wrong God, but maybe not, maybe the same God, maybe all the same God. And then the moment, the moment I will always remember, the moment that

I remember above all the others with this man. The moment that stands out. I remember really next to nothing else, nothing about him, just a little about the room, so very little about anything we talked about, but I'm piecing together what we must have said, what I must have said, what I feel I said, and then he tells me how God will take care of this, what God's plan for my life is, how God will make all of this right again:

"I believe God will give you a son."

I remember pausing at this. I think I stopped breathing. I write this sentence now, and I tell you, I tell you without any pretense, without any sense of the aesthetic, without any temptation to the dramatic: I stop breathing, I stop breathing *right now.*

I believe that this man believed deep in his heart that he was helping. And I believed in that moment that he was helping me as well. And I also believed in that moment that this would never happen, that I would never have a son.

You're likely wondering why I believed all of this at the same time. If any of this writing has a point, if I intend you to understand anything, I would so very much like you to understand how I could hold all of these thoughts in mind at the same time. I could. That doesn't surprise me. Not one bit. I want you too to understand the force of it all, the immense pressure of it all, the build up, the build up, the contradictions, but still the force of it all, so much so that even now, here it goes again, and I'm decades, literally fucking decades away from it all. This is the key to my life, it's how I understand, however contradictory it seems even to me at times, how I move through the world, even now, so many years, even decades later.

God would give me a son; I would never have a son.

To touch this, to touch this thing…. Yes, God would give me a son, that's the formula, that's the way that my uncle's derailment of my natural and God-ordained path toward happy marriage with a woman would be set back on course, would be made right and whole. The unnatural desires given to me by my uncle, the ways in which my sense of what is intimate, even pleasurable would be made right is by having a son to whom I could transfer appropriately all of the feelings of affection that can — and can *rightly* — exist between men. Love between men isn't forbidden. No, not at all! God wants fathers to love their sons. Not touch them inappropriately, no, but love them, nurture them, guide then, discipline them when needed, but only discipline as a sign of love. I needed that. I needed a son to show me that it was OK for men to be intimate, that a man could love another male being — but this time, in the right way, in the true way, in the one true, right way that God intended. All could — and would — be made right.

I don't think that this man understood how incredibly odd all of this sounds. God would give me a son to raise, and *the son would make it right.* Of course, he believed this: this is the story of God sending his only begotten son to be sacrificed for our sins. So of course God would send me a son to help me, guide me, put me back on the straight and narrow — even though I was, supposedly as the future father, the one who would be helping and guiding my son. Talk about transference. Protestants don't believe in transubstantiation, the actual presence of the body of Christ in the consecrated Host of Holy Communion, but what is this transference except a form of transubstantiation? My son, my future son, the promise of my future sanity and wholeness, would be the living and God-given flesh of my redemption. An actual son, in the flesh.

Of all the things that I remember, I remember this promise, but I also remember that I never was explicit about what I feared. I didn't tell this man, this counselor, that I feared that I might truly and deeply, deep down, be gay. I feared that I had bad thoughts, very bad thoughts, and that I'd actually experimented, just a little, but I didn't articulate those thoughts and activities as indicative of an identity. They were indicative instead of a botching, a twisting, a bending. (No wonder one now out-of-fashion term for homosexuals was "bent."). No, I was botched. And I could botch others just as I had been botched. What had been done to me could be done to others.

And so, even more, the overriding reason that I knew, deep down, that I most definitely would not have a son is that I knew that I would do to my son what had been done to me. I had been abused, and therefore I was going to abuse. It was only a matter of time.

***

Why did I think this? Why was I so convinced I would abuse others? More than any other truth about myself, more than my belief that I would be able to love another, I feared that I would abuse someone. After all, I was already abusing myself.

I've already written about the little tie-up games I'd play as a kid, and how my first orgasm occurred when I unexpectedly creamed my briefs while lying in front of the television in my bedroom, wriggling in the ropes and belts I'd wrapped around me. I thought I'd done something wrong, that there was something physically wrong with me. But it also felt so good. Bound and pleasured, my body pleasuring me. I was horrified. Something must be wrong. I'm doing something wrong. I would only learn later that so many of us, queer or not, are launched into consciousness of our sexuality, of the pleasures possible, of the skyrocketing delights of the body, with the booster rockets of shame.

I suppose that my having tied myself up and (coincidentally?) achieving my first orgasm may have cemented the bond, as it were, for me between pleasure and bondage. Score for classical conditioning. But perhaps something in me was destined to experience this complexly intertwined pleasure. Something older, something more grounding of the polymorphous perversity of my body being entrained along particular tracks and grooves, the circuits of pleasure and its close cousin pain drawn into a relational network that would involve being dominated, tied up, restrained, controlled — even if only by enacting a fantasy of superheroes suffering. For those were often the images flying through my prepubescent brain — Batman with his silky underwear over his tights and his boy Robin in his green panties bound and helpless, about to be roasted alive while tied together to the spit turning over the Joker's fiery pit. (You see the delight I still take in such images as I write them today, my language turning perversely poetic...).

But still, something deeper, something more shadowy. Blue images.

I can't only blame pop culture. Sure, I can blame it a little bit, and I will. I do. But... *blame?* Is that even the right word? Maybe *appreciate* and *resent* in complex and ever-shifting proportions. So much of what we see throughout our lives, the culture telling itself its story over and over again, reaffirming its values through every sitcom, commercial, billboard, cheesy pop song, writing on our bodies and minds the desires, the perverse implantations, that program our sense of self in the world, that subject us to the culture's desiring ministrations and cruel optimisms. You can tell I have studied this.

But as I've been writing these thoughts, I've also started thinking of something else. I'm starting to think about my father, something deeper, something more shadowy. Blue images.

I had a somewhat troubled stomach as a child, frequent cramps, even a duodenal ulcer at one point. I wasn't regular, often constipated. My father would at times give me enemas, which pretty much immediately forced a substantial crap out of my little body, a convulsive shit. To this day, I don't mind holding it a bit, and then enjoy the explosion out of my ass. I have never been much turned on by anal sex, and have rarely allowed anything up the shoot, as they say — a conditioning perhaps of my early adult exposure to toxic and homophobic media about AIDS. But as I think more on this insertion reluctance, I realize that I am more interested in what comes out of the ass. I'm not into scat (I think), but the release of the pent-up, the held in, the retained — that can feel extraordinary. But I'm also wondering too if, after all of these years, at least four decades and more, I'm resisting the insertion of the enema, the tip of the slender plastic tubing that my father would push up my little boy butt. And I wonder if he enjoyed pushing it up there.

I never — ever — thought about any of these enemas until Mack had to bring one home in preparation for a colonoscopy. And then it hit me.

I wonder if my father was a pedophile.

This is a wondering for which I do not have evidence. And like what I've said about my uncle, there's not much I can say to answer the question, was my father a pedophile? How many of us really know what someone else is thinking when they are with themselves alone, touching themselves, intimate with their own genitalia? Is there a more fundamental question about our alienation from each other? What turns us on, deep down, privately, that we don't talk about?

The question generates speculation. It is the engine of erotic imagination — not just in terms of what fuels our own particular kinks, what drives our desire, but perhaps also what drives our interest in others, in what turns other people on. My most intimate bully was always trying to get inside my head — and for just this reason. "That's what you want, isn't it?" Note that this is a *question*. It reveals a lack of surety. It's a calculated guess, but there's still some room for doubt here, some wiggle room, some sense that the bully might not have gotten this quite right. The question probes. It asserts, yes, but also hesitates as it approaches the void between us. No, Mr. Bully, you can't really and truly (if there ever is such a finality) know what turns me on. You might get close. You might dance around it as you attempt to seduce me into this romance, betting that I'm the kind who wants to be put in my place.

Did my father think that I might like the enema? Did he imagine me as anally receptive? Did it matter to him what I might want?

To pose these questions is to come as close as I know how to imagining, reconstructing, and then analyzing the scene of violation. I cannot know what my attacker was thinking — for that's how I imagine my father, as an attacker: he's assaulting my little body. But even in saying that, I'm deep in the throes of imagination. Perhaps I've gotten all of this totally wrong. I was constipated. He was trying to help.

But in the intervening years, different stories, feelings, experiences, ways of thinking, novels and films, conversations with others, a whole discourse of sexuality and violence — all of this presses on me, works through me, penetrates me, prompts me. And then my own experiences, my direct experiences with sexualized violence, with homophobia, with shame-inducing homophobia, making me ashamed, feeling shitty. A story begins to form. An interpretation accrues. I write accrue, and my spell-checker asks if I actually mean "accuse." The computer program vectors the return of the repressed; it is the voice that gently urges me toward an interpretation, a *determination*. This is the right word, isn't it? This is what you want, isn't it?

Accrual emerges slowly into accusation. Maybe my father was a pedophile. It's a totally unfair thing to accuse him of, to wonder about, when I otherwise have no evidence. But that's perhaps the point: the wondering is itself a bending, a turning, a twisting. Everything gets twisted in the aftermath of sexual violence.

I have only just begun telling this story. How can I know how it will end? Most days, most every day, I don't think it will.

***

PART TWO

Structures of Violation

Others have gone before, have written about abuse, sexual abuse, about the torture of children through the impositions of desire and the exercises of power on their bodies. Some, many, have surely suffered more than I have. Their stories claim our attention; they want to haunt us with their own haunted lives. We, the haunted, are connected at times, if we are connected at all, through the violences done to us, but hopefully not *only* through it, even if *at least* through it.

Sometimes I need a break from my own story. I need to know that others have suffered. I perversely wonder *how* they have suffered. And I am just as perversely comforted in this shared suffering. I'm shamefully comforted that it's sometimes worse for others.

I conceive of this book during a summer (2018) when my drive to work, to the store, to get a coffee is replete with accounts of women being sexually assaulted, often but not always on the job, their abusers now called out, some on trial, some going to jail. Larry Nassar, Bill Cosby, Harvey Weinstein. A scandal up the road at USC reverberates on my campus with heightened scrutiny of anything that remotely looks like sexual harassment. And that's a good thing. We need to be so much more aware.[1]

---

1   Accounts of these atrocities are numerous, readily available online. They were sparked by the #MeToo movement.

But I also wonder about my own listening. At one point, during reports of the sentencing phase of Nassar's trial, I can't quite pull myself away from hearing the testimony. One young woman after another comes forward to talk about the abuse, the inappropriate touching, the fondling, the violation. The most brutal testimonies to my ears are from those whose parents were *in the same room* as Nassar performed his various "examinations." It's all just fucking horrifying. And I listen. I can't not.

Or can I?

I tell myself that I'm bearing witness, that it's the responsibility of each of us to bear witness to atrocities that have for far too long been held in secret, kept quiet, even actively denied. Too many secrets, too many scandals waiting to emerge.

I am not in the least sexually titillated by such stories. That might seem an odd thing to say, and it is an odd sentence to write. But if you have been abused, you find yourself making such statements — assertions that arise from your own constant self-interrogation. Do I find this arousing? *Why* do I find this action, activity, thought, story, encounter stimulating? Is this appropriate? Might this become "appropriate" in a different context, or with a safe word?

I'm being neither snide nor snarky here, and again I feel the need to clarify my intentions, thinking of you as you read this and how you might be wondering what the hell I'm doing. But again, as I listen to the stories from these young women, catching myself going to turn off the radio and then refusing to do so, all but forcing myself to listen, I have to wonder *why?*

And one answer is, yes, I'm relieved frankly to know that there are others. Not in any way that I would've wished this awfulness, this terrible abuse on them. But I'm relieved to know that they are there, that they too can corroborate my feelings. But more importantly, that they can give voice to the self-doubts that become the internal litany of so many of our days. *Did this really happen? Am I crazy in thinking this happened? What's wrong with me? Why would he do this to me? Did I ask for this? Did I signal in any way that I wanted this? Did I deserve this?*

And then even more, a step or two further: *Am I wrong that it sometimes felt good? Am I wrong that I sometimes am aroused thinking about this?*

Because sometimes I am aroused. I'm going to violate you right now if you keep on reading. I'm sitting here in this public cafe, writing these words, enjoying the clacking of my fingers as they race across this little keyboard, shifting my pelvis a bit in my shorts, feeling my underwear, thinking of my uncle slipping a piece of ice down my little white briefs when I'm just five years old, me cackling with delight, outraged and excited all at the same time, or even more, my father slipping the tip of the enema up my little butt, me squirming, shifting my chair with the thought of the plastic tube creeping up my butt, and I feel a little twitching in my cock, not a full-blown erection, but a stirring as they say, a most definite stirring that I'm not denying but that in some perverse way I'm enjoying and that I'm enjoying writing about as these people pass by with their coffees, thinking that I'm hard at work on some productive task when I'm actually getting a little aroused at the thought that someone later will read this and wonder what fucking kind of twisted pervert I am.

A young man stops and sits at the coffee bar in front of me and I check out his ass as he arranges his computer, setting up his workstation, putting in his ear buds. He's wearing Doc Martens and I imagine licking them. They look new. I realize I am a cliche. I delight a little in the cliche. He's got to be in his twenties, stubbled, with glasses, the kind of cute nerd that I enjoy scoping out. My cock twitches a bit more.

I am bearing witness to my own perversion here. And I am bearing witness to how I'm calling this "perversion" because I don't want to lose you. Some of you want to run away from this. I'm taking you where you don't want to go. Some of you are understanding this, maybe nodding along. Some of you who are understanding this are also wanting to run away. Just because I've learned to sit with these thoughts and hold them gently doesn't mean that you have to.

Am I wrong that it sometimes felt good? Am I wrong that I sometimes am aroused thinking about this?

No, I tell myself, it's not wrong. That boy setting up his computer is never going to hear from me. And even if he did, even if I walked over, even if I called out, I would do so carefully, politely, engagingly. If I made a pass at him and he declined, I'd immediately move on. I wouldn't linger, I wouldn't stalk, I wouldn't sulk, I wouldn't press the point. I'd smile and move on, thanking him in my mind for at least considering me, however quickly. I wouldn't abuse him. Instead, I imagine the inevitability of my rejection, of necessity, perhaps as a way to prevent myself from going over there to initiate a conversation. I know that my likelihood of engaging him in any way is vanishingly small. Few of us are that bold.

And then I wonder if that's a good thing.

But I can't be sorry for checking him out. And I'm learning not to be sorry or feel shame or degrade myself for thinking back with some pleasure on my uncle slipping a piece of ice down my underpants. Perhaps he was grooming me. Perhaps the play was innocent. Perhaps I misremember this incident. All of the "perhapses" here become part of the friction of intimacies and desires that we move through in making contact with one another.

It's so hard to know what someone is thinking.

So, perhaps again, in thinking of this boy across from me as my cock is twitching at the thought of that ice cube sliding up against my ass crack, I'm delighting in my imagining of someone who can't know what I'm imagining as a way of approaching the black box of my uncle's own imagination, not knowing what he thought or felt himself as he crept up behind me, fingering the elastic of my little white briefs. Was his cock twitching in that moment?

Does it matter if it was?

I can't know, I don't know. I will never know. But I must still ask that question. If he never actually abused me, if he only ever slid that ice cube down my shorts and his cock responded for just a fraction, coming close to the body of a young boy but pulling back, playfully approaching the body of a young boy, asserting his dominance over it for just a moment, but pulling back to laugh at the play, to note my own boyish delight — if that's all that happened in that moment and his cock twitched just a little bit, does it matter?

These are the questions you ask yourself. These are the questions you ask *about yourself.*

***

I'm writing this just days after the *Houston Chronicle* has reported on the alleged abuse of seven hundred children over twenty years in southern baptist congregations. Comparisons to the abuses perpetrated by catholic priests abound. The Southern Baptist Convention blames the relative autonomy of their churches, the much vaunted freedom that characterizes protestant faiths as opposed to the stricter hierarchies of catholicism. But what's clear is that many church "fathers," like their catholic counterparts, knew of the abuses and covered them up, or ignored them, or chose not to report them, or advised forgiveness and reconciliation.[2]

I read this paragraph over and over again, and then again:

They left behind more than 700 victims, many of them shunned by their churches, left to themselves to rebuild their lives. Some were urged to forgive their abusers or to get abortions.

Urged to forgive their abusers or get abortions. Urged to forgive their abusers or get abortions.

I read this again. I get stuck in this paragraph. I am trapped inside this paragraph, or that's how it feels. But no, it's not just how it feels. I *am* trapped here. *Urged to forgive their abusers or get abortions.* Urged. Forgive. Everything that's possibly wrong with christianity is right here, in these sentences, just these two sentences. They left behind more than seven hundred victims, many of them shunned by their churches, left to themselves to rebuild their lives. Some were urged to forgive their abusers or to get abortions. Shame. Abortions. Forgiveness. Urged to forgive. I am trapped in this paragraph. I am trapped.

I was not sexually abused by a baptist minister. I was sexually abused by *every* baptist minister. There is no contradiction here, even as I want to make clear that the physical, emotional, sex-

---

2 The *Houston Chronicle* article was published online February 10, 2019, https://www.houstonchronicle.com/news/investigations/article/Southern-Baptist-sexual-abuse-spreads-as-leaders-13588038.php.

ual, and spiritual assault that these young people encountered, that they endured on their bodies, minds, and souls, that their violation by people whom they should have been able to trust, the evisceration of their faith in people who were supposed to shepherd them, guide them, *love them* — these victims know a particularity of abuse that cuts me to the quick, that I can barely write about because it is so inconceivably awful and destructive and life-changing. They know a dimension of abuse that I can only acknowledge, that I choose to witness, that I must witness because so few have chosen to, because so many have chosen to turn away.

I was not sexually abused by a baptist minster in the way they were. But I was abused by every baptist minister — because their entire church polity has decided that people like me must be turned away, that I am the kind of person consigned to the sulfurous fires of hell for all of eternity, that AIDS is only the faintest glimmerings of divine justice for faggots, for faggots, for faggots, for people who, historically, were justly burned alive, burned alive, burned alive for their damnable sins. Baptist ministers left behind more than seven hundred victims, many of them shunned by their churches, left to themselves to rebuild their lives. No. No, baptist ministers have left behind countless believers, countless numbers, countless faggots just like me, shunned by their churches, left to rebuild their lives, left to rebuild their lives. My aunt, a baptist woman, a devout believer, saying, saying in all the honesty of faith she could muster, like Jerry Falwell and others, that Hurricane Katrina was God's punishment for the homosexuals on Bourbon Street. Shunned by their churches, left to rebuild their lives. Shunned. Shamed. I tell my former baptist pastor, a man I once admired, a man I once loved, that I am gay, and he tells me, writes me in an email, how sorry he is, how sorry he is, and that people today think too much about the journey and not enough about the destination. Because he knows, he doesn't have to say it, he knows, and I don't have to hear him say it, that my destination is hell, that I'm going straight to hell, to burn in the sulfurous fires of eternal damnation. I am going to hell. Damned. Shamed. Shamed now. They left behind more than seven hundred victims, many of them shunned by their churches, left to themselves to rebuild their lives. But more than seven hundred, so many more than seven hundred. Shamed. Shunned. Left behind.

I was not sexually abused by a baptist minister in the way that these seven hundred were. But I will stand with them in the fires of hell. I will stand with them. I acknowledge them. I see them. I see *you*, shamed, shunned, left behind. We will stand together in the fires of hell, in the howling winds of the eternal hurricane blowing us away from the faithful, cleansing the world of our sin. I see you. I am with you. I was not sexually abused by a baptist minister in the same way you were. But we all, all of us, were abused by *every* baptist minister.

***

I listen to Annie Lennox sing "Why" over and over again. *Turning me inside out.* These thoughts still turning me inside out. I'm listening in the days after the shooting of gay brothers at the Pulse Nightclub in Orlando, Florida. Just a fraction of all of the shootings in this country, but this time an assault on people like me, people like me, no matter what the news says.[3]

My mother calls, a friend in New York texts. They want to know if I'm OK. I wasn't there, I wasn't anywhere near there. But I am everywhere where people like me are, where they are assaulted, where they are hunted down and killed. Where their lives are turned inside out. Where boys who love boys are thrown off of buildings by fundamentalists, by religious fundamentalists. I try to explain to a colleague why I can't accept that invitation to speak in Beirut, a place I would otherwise love to visit. But I can't. I can't. I can't explain. *You don't know what I fear.* You don't. You think you know, but you don't know what I fear. You can't know. You can't know it unless you live like I do.

Why, but why. Why, Annie sings, and I know that she's singing or someone she's thinking about is singing, someone whom she imagines singing this song, is signing about something deeply personal, a love lost, a love that isn't working out, a love that she brings down to the water's edge so they can cast away these doubts. But I know this song as something else, something more, something more than the personal. This is about every boy who loves another boy and is thrown off the top of a building, about boys dancing with boys being gunned down in a nightclub in Orlando. This is about asking why, why, and *can we go down to the water's edge, can we cast away these doubts,* but we can't, we can't, and *some feelings are better left unsaid, but they still turn me inside out.*

This boat is sinking, this boat is sinking. You don't know what I fear. You can't know what I fear. Some of you know what

---

3 See p. 33, fn. 3 about Annie Lennox's *Diva,* on which "Why" is included. Accounts of the Orlando Nightclub Shooting, as it's called, on June 12, 2016, are readily available online.

I fear, and I'm so sorry for you, I'm so very sorry for you. I wish it weren't so. I wish things were different.

On Sunday after the shooting I go to a gallery to talk about art and what it can do, about the power of art in dark times. I don't know what to say, but I talk about the power of art in dark times. I want to believe in it. Later that same Sunday I go to get my hair cut and the boy cutting my hair is so gentle I could cry. I want to be taken care of. I wish things were different. And then I think that the Latin queers dancing at Pulse were at the forefront of what it means to be in the West, the best we have to offer of self-determination, of asserting your right to love, of everything that is truly progressive and forward-thinking in an otherwise botched and toxic culture. So of course they were a target. But the news says they weren't. They weren't a target because they were gay. But I know better. Some of you know better.

I think many of the boys and girls dancing there must have hated themselves, like I hated myself, like I still hate myself. But I also know that they were the best we have to offer, the very best an otherwise botched and toxic culture has to offer. Do I contradict myself? So I contradict myself. You don't know what I feel. You can't. But some of you do. And I'm so sorry, so very sorry.

***

I couldn't help but think that I had been here before. This wasn't the first time I'd contacted my school. Over the years, as I had received in the mail various updates on the school's activities, and as I had even been called by alumni asking for donations to help keep the mission of the school going, I had talked back, telling alumni, some of whom I remembered as classmates, that no, no, no I wasn't going to be giving any of my money to XXX, that I did not believe in the mission of the school. I even emailed the principal at one point after receiving multiple mailings about a fundraising campaign, saying that I would consider making a contribution if the school set up a "gay-straight student alliance," to assist those students who were wondering about their sexuality and feeling in need of support, or at least friendly faces. The principal actually emailed me back saying that such would not be in keeping with the dictates of the catholic faith. A honest reply. One I expected and knew well.

I thought back further and realized how long I'd been waging this battle, hoping for a different outcome. And then I found in my files this letter that I had typed up and sent on my former college employer's letterhead:

May 16, 1994

Dear Brother —

After careful consideration, meditation, and prayer, I have decided to write this letter to you in the hopes that you will consider my thoughts in this time of transition and growth for XXX. I am writing to you in particular because you seem to be in charge of the school's current reorganization (if that is not too strong a word), but my remarks should not be limited to you alone; I intend these comments for all who have an interest in the future development of the school.

It has been almost ten years since I graduated from XXX, and those years have been full of exciting change for me. I have been so preoccupied with educating myself, developing new relationships, and establishing myself professionally that I have not often thought of my high school days. This lack of recollection is due to some extent to the fact that one's teenage years are often a painful time, a time, I'm sure, that many young men are glad to move on from in anticipation of the adult challenges life has to offer.

Recently, however, I cannot help but think that a large part of my desire to put distance between myself and my years at XXX stems from several very disturbing experiences I had during high school. In my case, the usual teenage turmoil was aggravated by an unfortunate series of events that I hope and pray were (and are) particular to me alone.

Allow me to enumerate for the sake of clarity:

1. *I was a painfully shy and quiet teenager, not especially athletic. I mostly kept to myself and was rather bookish. These, however, were not traits in vogue, and I was often ridiculed and made fun of. Most painful, and (sadly) most prevalent, was the fact that most of my classmates considered me a "fag" — and they did not hesitate to tell me so. Besides the usual verbal taunts, I often found obscene notes addressed to me in my locker, and my mannerisms became the source for much imitation and "physical comedy." In short, I became known as the "class queer" — a labeling I now consider sexually abusive. But my point in telling you this story is not to vent my frustrations for actions almost a decade old; boys will be boys, and humiliating others is an unfortunate characteristic of so many young men. No, my concern is not for the young people who taunted and teased me, but for the teacher who "got in on the game" as well. Several classmates, including a few whom I considered friends, reported that a particular teacher had referred to me as the "class fag" during one of his classes; although I hope this did not occur, the number of people who reported it to me on different occasions makes me suspect it is unfortunately true.*

2. *This teacher's actions were not idiosyncratic, and the number of poor educators I encountered during high school was staggering. Again, allow me to enumerate:*

   (a) One teacher routinely awarded extra credit to students because they wore particular articles of clothing. I was often

made fun of in this class — by the teacher — because I did not comply.

[...]

(e) Another teacher asked me to tutor him in German, a language I'm particularly strong in. He offered to pay me per hour and asked me to keep a running record of how much time we spent in tutorials together. After ten hours of tutoring the teacher refused to see or pay me for my efforts. He became "fluent" in avoiding me.

[...]

I could list other instances, but I don't want to sound petty. In fact, some of these may sound peevish to you, but I urge you to consider how such instances of unfairness and even cruelty could appear to an adolescent already alienated from most of his classmates. Lacking a supportive peer group, I could seldom find comfort, fairness, or consistency among a group of educators we were told to respect and look up to.

Many teenagers are mistreated during high school; such is part and parcel of growing up and living in an often violent and abusive society. What disheartens me is the remarkably bad role-modeling I was offered at XXX. Regardless of the students' treatment of me, the poor examples I was given by adults and teachers have been some of the most disturbing and lasting lessons I have learned about life.

Since graduating from XXX, I have completed a Ph.D., married, and taken a position at YYY. I am a published scholar and composer, fellow for a Washington think tank, highly regarded teacher, and director of music for the church my wife and I are members of. I have not allowed the negative attitudes and actions of students and teachers alike to prevent me from attaining a high degree of personal and professional achievement.

Certainly, there are a few teachers I remember at XXX who attempted to be encouraging and supportive. Not all educators are as deceitful and petty as some of the teachers I encountered; what is sad is that I encountered so many. I do not know if these people are still employed at XXX, and I am certainly not making a case for their dismissal. But I urge you to create an environment *for students and teachers which engenders tolerance and decency, fairness and Christian behavior. XXX claims to be a Christian school; I am glad that my experiences did not turn me away from either Christianity or education. It would have been so easy to become bitter and resentful; fortunately, I am neither, and I hope that my concern for XXX as an educational institution has been apparent.*

I will conclude with a caveat. It may be, as some would argue, that I would not have accomplished so much in my life in such a short time if I'd not had so much adversity to overcome. On the other hand, what could I have accomplished had I had a supportive, caring, and nurturing environment? As a professional educator, I invite you to consider this question — even as I continue to consider it in relation to each of my own students on a daily basis.

Sincerely,
Jonathan Alexander, Ph.D.[4]

Looking back at this letter, I find it remarkable for a few reasons. First and foremost, I was clearly willing to use some "straight" privilege to assert the unjustness of my abuse, particularly homophobic abuse. I wanted this brother to know that they — students and teachers — had gotten me wrong; they'd misjudged me, and only an act of divine grace prevented my path from being fully perverted into homosexuality. Certainly, damage had been done; why else compose such a letter and send it a decade later? But the maximum possible damage, a homosexual life, had been avoided. Thank god. But even more, I know in my heart, even though I am perhaps less explicit about this in the letter itself, that I wanted not just to mark unprofessional behavior but hoped that the brother would think through to the insinuation that such behavior (tempting students to dress the way the brother in question desired) constituted potentially

---

4   I've obviously left some parts of this letter out, in large part because some items don't seem as pressing as they must have to me at the time I originally wrote and sent it.

sketchy sexual behavior. And the teacher who wanted German lessons... hmmm, what else might he have wanted? I remember him sitting close to me during his tutelage, his leg pressing against mine. What was going on there? What perhaps did he want to "teach" *me*? While I might have held back from the more intense accusations I was tempted to make, but I left some bread crumbs.

I also used my christianity as another form of privilege. At the time, I was the music director for a United Church of Christ congregation, that fairly liberal branch of christianity, so much so that some folks in the church quipped that UCC actually stood for Unitarians Considering Christianity. Some UCC churches are "open and affirming" of queer people, and while I wasn't queer-identified at the time, I was clearly moving away from associations with catholicism and the Southern Baptist Convention, and more toward a kind of religious or spiritual practice that was, frankly, less toxic, if still associated with the millennia-old institutions that have damaged — and killed — so many people like me. But even though I was slowly, oh so slowly, prying ugly horned hands of dogmatic belief off me, I couldn't resist the temptation to throw a bit of Jesus in this brother's face. *See? I'm being Christ-like, offering the hand of forgiveness while calling bullshit on your school's claim to Christian education. I survived you, thanks be to god.*

In my defense — and I do feel I need to defend myself — I was committed both to my marriage and my christianity. Yes, I had questions, about both. And yes, I shared those questions with my wife and with those close to me in the church. I wasn't exactly faking here. But still, guilty: I used straight and christian privilege to chastise this brother, to use him as the whipping boy for what had been done to me, for the various ways in which I had been violated, and continued to feel violated, by this place, this time.

But maybe the most remarkable bit of the letter to me now is this sentence: "Many teenagers are mistreated during high school; such is part and parcel of growing up and living in an often violent and abusive society." The semicolon joins the two statements in an unexamined relationship, yoking them together as though they are just naturally a part of one another: kids hurt each other because they grow up in an "abusive society." I already identified earlier in the letter the bullying as "sexually abusive." I was clearly thinking about and ramping up my own understanding — and rhetoric — of what had happened to me. But, in this particular letter, I'm not quite probing the wound, and the larger wound of masculinity. I'm still willing to say that "boys will be boys, and humiliating others is an unfortunate characteristic of so many young men." But why? *Why is that so?* What is being acted out? What gendered trauma, unexplored or unacknowledged, manifests in such cruelty? Without a doubt, as I look back on this letter now, I'm about to make the connections that are important, that are vital: we are all growing up in a culture that is abusing us, that violates us at our softest spots of pleasure, and this should come as no surprise to anyone who understands christianity as the religion of a god willing to sacrifice his only son and demands — *demands* — that that sacrifice occur as the only pathway of reconciliation.

I have come to different realizations later in life. Our culture hates children. We eat our young. We mortgage our present into their future, requiring that they bear the burden of all of our sins, paying for our mistakes, inheriting the world that we continue to damage and that we will require them to live in. They may not survive it. We don't seem to care. Of course our god killed his son. He is only doing what we have asked of our own children, that they die for us, that they be sacrificed for our needs, so we can sleep a bit more comfortably at night. We don't think of where they will need to sleep.

So no, I'm not surprised that I'm not quite there yet in this letter, that I'm not quite realizing that boys hurting boys need not be natural, need not be the order of things. I have a context in mind — a violent and abusive society — but I'm not pushing hard enough yet. And that may be where my cloaking in my marriage and my christianity prevented me from seeing more fully what I was only beginning to catch a glimpse of.

I actually received a response to this letter. The brother from the school wrote a comparably long, three-page missive full of apology and a stated desire to do better. I did not know this brother when I was in high school, and I don't think he works there now; in fact, I don't think any of the brothers live on campus anymore, and the school is run predominantly by laypeople. This brother might not even be alive anymore; I saw a picture of him and he was already an old man by the time he wrote me.

But he responded. I won't reproduce his entire letter, though I note that it is dated May 28, so written pretty much immediately upon receipt of my letter. And it begins by saying "I am sorry I wasn't here when you had tried to contact me by telephone." I have no recollection of trying to call this brother. I can't imagine what I would've said, how I might have vocalized anything in the letter to this stranger. But apparently I tried to call. Or did I? I really don't remember, or have any sense of what I might have been thinking in making, much less considering, such a call. Writing seemed so much the safer way to proceed.

The brother calls me "thoughtful" in sharing some of my "experiences via the typed letter. No doubt, in doing so, you must have relived both positive and negative feelings?!" Really? Yes, indeed. He then apologizes for how I was treated, and while he acknowledges my acknowledgment of the "part and parcel" he also says, rightly, that "there is no reason for the negative role-modeling you experienced at XXX." Such behavior, particularly on the part of the teachers, "violates the core principles of the Christian Brother tradition." I catch a little breath at this word, violates. *Violates.* But what — not who — is violated here. The tradition, his tradition. He acknowledges a violation has occurred. But not against me. Against the tradition. His tradition.

The brother says he is sharing my letter with some other "key people" and is even using it "as a basis to make the point that with all the positive change taking place at XXX, it is so very important to continually cultivate and develop a Christian atmosphere. Admittedly this is a very real challenge in the '90s." I don't know what this means. The '90s? The brother then goes on to laud the new principal, a layperson, who will make the "tough" decisions about putting the school on the right and godly path. And, most importantly, "There is without question a clear emphasis on the importance of religious values." And there I need to stop. I can't go on. I couldn't go on. Within a couple of years, I will have left the church, any christian church, even the mild-mannered and tolerant United Church of Christ, declared myself at least bisexual, taken on the mantle of queer activism, divorced, started dating men, and moved away with a man I love.

I don't blame this brother for my decisions. There's nothing to blame. I was violated. I live with it. I live in it. I survive it. And at times, I'm overwhelmed by it, by all of it.

* * *

You'll want to know about the woman I'm about to marry, and I'm not going to tell you much. There are many reasons for this, but primarily because I don't want to tell someone else's story. And her story is very much her own story, one that I suspect she's been working on for some time. To tell it, or a chunk of it, seems a gross violation, and perhaps precisely the kind of violation that I want to avoid because it's been done to me so many times. Indeed, in so many ways, others have offered me bits and pieces of my story, inviting me to think of my life in particular ways, to adopt a version of my self that makes sense to them, to consider how their narrative logics might help me understand what my own life adds up to. Each of these offerings and invitations is a kind of violation. It's a telling of my story for me, a bending of the arc of my narrative into tales that are more comfortable for others, that seem *right* to them. But they are not always right for me.

The problem I'm facing as I write this is that I will, inevitably, violate others in the telling of my own tale. I will characterize others, impersonate them, lodge them into my story in ways that will not make sense for their own lives. Most impertinently, I will speak for the dead, who no longer have a voice with which to correct my version or object to my assertions. But still, I will nonetheless allow myself to speak most freely for the dead. I won't regret that much, and you may understand why in time, or you might be able to glean from your own stories the necessity of violating the dead to make your own life possible. But the living I will attempt to honor, as they are still here to tell us their side of things. And they should.

With all of that said, I still do not believe I know everything, even about my own story. I am not always a master of my own narrative. And that is very much part of the problem.

So: I am about to marry this woman, and later in life my friends will ask me, "When did you know?" "Know what?" I will ask back. "Well, you know, that you were gay?" Asking this question is a violation. You should never ask someone when they "knew" they were gay unless they start talking to you about their theories on the origin, etiology, and trajectory of their emergent queerness.

Part of what violates me when I'm asked such a question is the assumption on the part of my friends, sometimes strangers, that I somehow made a mistake in getting married to a woman. That, given a different world, another time, I would absolutely have made another, better choice. If, say, I'd met this woman in 2018 as opposed to 1989, I would unequivocally have known that, nope, she is off limits, you will not marry her, you *should* not marry her, keep moving, you'll find a man to marry in time. This is the narrative that most people, even now, in a supposedly more enlightened and tolerant time vis-à-vis issues of non-heteronormative sexuality — this is the narrative that most people are comfortable with. Gays marry gays. Straights marry straights. And when something happens that looks like a different way of telling this story, then it must be questioned, even labeled. *That is clearly a mistake.*

I'm sitting across from a relatively new friend, a colleague with whom I was hired and with whom I will work very closely over the next decade plus. We are at a children's birthday party. I don't have children, and I note that I will not really be invited back to birthday parties for children in the future. My long-term male partner is with me. We are not yet married because it isn't legal yet, but, by the time of this story, we had been together for over ten years. We are still together today, and now legally married. I have to remind myself sometimes that I'm on my second marriage, it's just been that long.

At the time, though, I remembered more of that first marriage, and I would casually at times in polite conversation refer to my ex-wife. Nothing scandalous, just a small marker of a past life. So, at this birthday party, for instance, I say something like, "Oh yes, Colorado is lovely for skiing. I first went with my wife in '94, and we had a great time — a great time, that is, until I couldn't figure out how to stop on a particularly long run and ended up with pants full of snow..." I'm obviously responding to something someone said, but I'm no fool. As soon as I say something about my wife, perhaps even seconds before, I know that I'm revealing something about myself that is going to unsettle, that will hiccup the conversation.

As I think of it, I realize that I am violating the protocols of polite conversation, which is one of the reasons I suspect that people will not invite me to future birthday parties for their children. Note: I do not in the moment think that I am saying anything scandalous. But I am definitely marking myself as someone not totally inclined to follow the prescribed script. Gays go with gays. Straight with straights.

My new friend and colleague notes that hiccup with raised eyebrows. "Jonathan! I didn't know you'd been married..." Well, why would you have? We've practically just met. I affect a kind of mild disdain. His comment doesn't explicitly state that I've violated the script but he's definitely implied it. And others lean in to hear my response.

"Well, yes, I was."
"And?"
"And what?"
"Did she know you were gay?"

It's at this point that I think that I'm likely getting what I deserved. Gay goes with gay. Violation elicits with violation. I knew what I was doing. I detoured the conversation. I decided not to play by the rules. And now people are asking questions. I have violated their sense of how the world works, and now they feel free to violate me, to begin asking questions that are very personal, that are not easy to answer, that can only produce additional discomfort for all involved.

But I can't be entirely sorry. I have momentarily complicated things for people. I have upset their sense of how things work. At this point, I want their understanding of intimacy and even the erotic to be a little bit more... hmmm, how to says this: I want their understanding to be just a bit more. But it is upsetting. And I've learned that I have to live with some of the discomfort of pushing these boundaries, especially if I'm going to do so at a new colleague's child's birthday party, where we are celebrating the product of a traditional marriage.

Still, I feel violated. And I begin to wonder if part of what I'm doing isn't just a queer public service, expanding people's sense of intimate possibilities. I begin to wonder if part of what I'm doing is spreading the sense of violation, offering it to others, sharing it with others, inviting them to participate in my ongoing sense of discomfort.

I note, as I write this, the words I use: I'm back to offering and inviting. A conversational bomb, though, isn't an invitation.

It's a violation.

***

I've been listening recently to podcasts and interviews with Eileen Myles, the extraordinary American poet, someone I've always thought of in my mind as a *lesbian* poet and writer, author of classics such as *Chelsea Girls,* an exploration of the lives, loves, and losses of young women in New York. Focusing on what the narrator calls her "lesbianity," *Chelsea Girls* is a kind of autobiographical fiction, or autofiction, loosely based on Myles's own experiences ranging from life with an alcoholic father to her attempts to make it as a poet in the city in the 1970s. I say "she" and "her" because at the time Myles used the female pronouns for self-identification. More recently, though, she's started using they, so I should say that they now prefer to be referred to with the increasingly accepted "they" to mark, in the singular, gender neutrality, an identification as non-binary, or a refusal to mark or signify gender. This doesn't mean that Myles, as of this writing, is trans identified, but it does mean that they honor the pluralities of their gender experience.

As Myles puts it in a couple of different interviews, such as the *Bookworm* one with Michael Silverblatt, whom they gently and gracefully correct at the end of the interview (*just try once saying "they," Michael*), they started to understand themselves as "they" when they heard the story of Jesus casting out a demon, asking its name, and hearing the reply: "I am Legion."[5] The poor man whom Jesus is trying to help is apparently infested with not just one, not just two, but a whole hellish host of demonic beings. For Myles, though, the story is one of multiplicity, say, along the lines of Walt Whitman proclaiming that "I contain multitudes." At one level, they are gesturing to how all of us contain multiple selves inside, even as we attempt, normatively, to understand ourselves as singular and unified beings. But, more particularly, Myles is appreciating their own experience of walking down the street or into a bakery and being variously and sometimes simultaneously referred to as both sir and ma'am.

---

5   This episode of *Bookworm* aired on November 8, 2018 and is available here: https://www.kcrw.com/culture/shows/bookworm/eileen-myles-evolution.

They are plural. They contain, perform, and are experienced as different genders at the same time.

I love this, in no small part because I've always had a thing for butch lesbians, particularly those whose gender performance (and it's not always "performance," just their being in the world, their going about their daily business) often confuses people who "naturally" (that is, normatively) just assign gender as part of *their* daily business in the world, how they go about their days. (Treading carefully here, I don't want to identify Eileen Myles as a butch lesbian. But I bet they have been identified as such, and has likely identified as such themself.) I've seen this confusion up close. Having dinner with my friend Jackie, we are sometimes mistaken as a gay couple on a date. Jackie is largely used to this, if not at times a bit put out about it, and I think we both sort of thrill to the misrecognition when we are out together. But it's also a violation, Jackie's gender being *read* and *assigned* and *mistaken,* her womanhood and its complexity reduced to a labeling that is wrong precisely because it's reductive of the complexity of gender.

The emergence of "they" as a way for people who don't want their gender assigned could become a way for folks to avoid mis-assigning in the first place. I myself am trying to get into the habit of not only referring to people as "they" when they request that I do but also referring to people whose gender I don't know as "they" — until I'm corrected. I like the radicality here — that idea that something once so codified, essential, and *sure* of itself like gender is now a matter of self-determination, and that we should all wait to be *told* what pronouns are at play before just assuming that we sit so comfortably in the world that we can assign gender to everyone around us. That's a generative kind of discomfort to me — one that works against the assigning of gender as a *primary kind of violation* that so many of us experience, and that relocates the ability of people to understand and express something so seemingly fundamental as gender to those of us who are disciplined by it — which would be, actually, *all of us.*

But I also love Myles's reference to the demonic legion because they embrace the story as a primarily *positive* one. Jesus is depicted as casting out a legion of demons, which we are to understand as a necessary act of cleansing. Myles though loves the legion and sees the casting out as the problem. We should embrace our multiplicity. The former christian in me absolutely thrills to this rereading of a well-known biblical narrative, and even today writing this recap feels a bit heretical. It's a violation of a sacred story, albeit one that, as Myles would tell it, is actually a story about the violation of our multiplicity, an attempt to cast out our complexity and reduce us to simpler, manageable units. Fuck that, they say.

Now, here comes the hard part. I thrill to Myles's rereading, reinterpretation, even scandalous misreading. Queers have often had to misread the stories we've inherited, the stories that circulate so powerfully in our culture but that also fail to imagine and sometimes even attempt to eradicate our existence. The stories that seek to cast us out. So misreading is a powerful strategy for finding ourselves in stories and not just recognizing ourselves but also valuing, honoring, and even creating ourselves. Queers do this work all the time *just to stay alive*.

But the stories that circulate are sometimes hard to misread. They shout at us, screaming. We can't help but hear them. Their voices are everywhere, interpenetrating our being. They make us. The work of not hearing them, much less trying to hear them differently, is extraordinarily difficult at times. Hell, it is difficult at *most* times.

Put another way, those stories that scream to us about who we are or that tell us we are *wrong* — those stories that then become a part of our being because we've heard them for so very long, because we were raised on them, because they were with us at the very moment when we took our first breaths (you are a boy, you are a girl) — those stories are our fundamental violation. They are an ontology of identity that is basically abusive, a penetration of the self by others from the very beginning of our lives, without our consent. They mark our flesh and our psyches, shaping them so that we believe them, sometimes not even fully aware that we hold beliefs (and beliefs that are toxic to our survival) because they so penetrate — and, in the process, constitute — us.

***

I spend part of the afternoon with a friend in downtown Los Angeles, a delightful brunch, catching up, rehearsing and reviewing the kinks of anxiety that mar both of our lives. A kindred spirit. We've known each other for years.

Walking off his hamburger and my complex hipster egg dish, plus two tequila cocktails, we find ourselves behind a young couple, black woman and white man, both cute, pawing each other as they stroll along, clearly in love or lust or maybe both. Then the woman unselfconsciously spanks his ass and shoves her fist up his butt, while he gently, playfully swats at her hand to get her to stop. I can't help but wonder what secrets are revealed here, what little kinky play was referenced. Does he like to take it up the ass, or enjoy a little butt play, having his plump behind swatted, the bad bad boy? We won't know. I'm totally projecting. They drift around the corner, still talking, laughing, pawing each other.

I head to Union Station to take the train back to Orange County and then see a young male couple, both white, arms interlocked, walking through the underground tunnel connecting different parts of the station. It's crowded, plenty of people around. They don't seem to care. I think to myself again: *they don't care* that anyone sees them. And why should they? What does it matter, in this city of angels, two young men, walking arm-in-arm. We pass each other and they are conscious of me conscious of them. I must scream "gay" in my little copper shorts and my vinyl sneakers. I always go a little extra gay when visiting my friend David, another gay man, in downtown LA. But there's nothing more than consciousness of my presence on their part, a brief acknowledgment that they see me, another gay man.

I must admit that for me, there's perhaps more *self-consciousness* than not, more than just an acknowledgment, more like a calling out, and I wonder how exposed I'm making myself, how visible, how much a *target*. Yes, I have gotten to a point where I'm starting to feel safe being more visibly gay, but only in bits and spurts, for small stretches of time in very particular places. My primary inclination otherwise is still to hide. I can't help but think that, with this couple and the earlier one in lust, they are experiencing a world I never have — a world in which they can more explicitly — and without much self-consciousness—express themselves intimately. Theirs is a world I likely never will inhabit, at least not comfortably in my own skin.

Without a doubt, the straight couple enjoy their straight privilege, but people *have* fought for interracial relationships to be a thing that isn't much noticed. And more recently, gays and lesbians have fought so that these two boys can walk not just next to each other *but as a couple* in a public place. These young people come largely *after* the fight. Surely, other fights lie ahead, and we can always regress. I fear more often than not these days, in the second year of the Trump presidency, that we are regressing, that the possibility of further regression is likely. But for now, these couples live in the world, in their bodies, in ways that I never could as a child. They live in ways that would feel strange to me even now. My husband and I do at times hold hands in public. We sometimes even kiss. But not often. Rarely, even. And mostly only in places that are explicitly marked as "gay." It's obvious we are a couple. I appreciate that obviousness. But what I miss, what I don't have, what I'm likely never to experience, is the sheer animal delight in bodies, in the public display of affection, that these young couples experience.

Again, there are differences. I bet the gay couple wouldn't be playfully fisting one another in public. There are limits after all, even in a city of angels. But they already feel, at least to me, so much further ahead in their lives, in the pleasure of their lives, in the demand to take and make and experience pleasure in their lives. I envy them. I applaud them. I love them in my own way.

I wish them all the luck in the world.

I wish them never to experience the insecurity I feel in my own body. I wish that they never experience the discomfort when someone flirts with them, wondering if it's really meant for them, wondering what's wrong with the person flirting. There's this lovely kid in a coffee shop I go to. Young, boyish. He wears overalls with fanciful shirts, and a baseball cap, just like a kid would. From the moment I started going to this particular coffee shop, he's flirted a bit. Teased me once when I walked in with a Title Boxing hoodie on, wondering if I boxed, saying that he thinks he could still take me even if I did box. He's flirting. It's obvious to anyone. Even I start to see it, but I don't respond. I can't. And it's not just that I'm married. Mack wouldn't mind. Mack would probably like to see this flirtation in action. But I stall, I equivocate. I don't need to do anything but just smile and play along. But I'm more business than pleasure. *Yes, the dark roast please.* And so, in time, he stops flirting. And I feel the loss of it, the loss of it all, my inability to engage in this simple social convention, a little flirty banter, a little bit of play. It's a loss. Something not just lost but taken from me. Sometime I deny myself because, deep down, I don't think I deserve it. Deep down, pleasures should be taken *from me,* not offered to me, not given generously, not proffered with some banter.

I sit with my coffee and brood. I want to do better. I want to try harder. I want to play along. But it's so much effort. A few tears come to my eyes, and I'm ashamed. I'm fifty-one. It won't be getting better. None of this is going to get any better.

***

I'm writing this just after hearing reports of the alleged homophobic and racist attack on actor Jussie Smollett, an openly gay Black man, who was accosted in the early morning in Chicago by a couple of men. This story will change in time, but right now I am reacting to the report as though it is all too real, not just a story on the news, not just a story that someone might have been made up for whatever reason. In the moment, in the moment of its reporting, it's real. According to CNN, "The attackers allegedly yelled 'racial and homophobic slurs' and 'poured an unknown chemical substance on the victim,' police said." Apparently the unknown chemical substance was bleach. The slurs included the n-word and faggot. The attackers also apparently shouted "This is MAGA country" at the beaten star, around whose neck they had put a rope. Some commentators and politicians, such as Kamala Harris, Democratic senator from California and, at the time, 2020 presidential contender, called the assault a modern-day lynching.[6]

The dual violations of racism and homophobia are unimaginable to me — in part, of course, because as a white man I do not know what it's like to walk down the street as a Black man in this culture, in what passes for a culture that's been built on the bloodied ground of Indigenous and Black peoples, peoples whom we have yet to acknowledge fully as human beings. This attack occurs barely a week after the "stand off" between the white MAGA-capped teen boy and an Indigenous elder. This is the United States we currently inhabit. This is the United States that is not only not ready to acknowledge the past sufferings inflicted on Indigenous and Black peoples in the course of building white democracy; it's an America that seems intent on reminding them that they are still less than human.

All of this is shameful, appalling, atrocious, but people like me are currently forced to recognize that it is so from *our* perspective. There are others who clearly, for whatever complex po-

---

6 Accounts of the incidents surrounding and involving Jussie Smollett are readily available online. As of this writing in 2021, attempts to understand what happened are still evolving.

litical or psychological reasons, are not appalled. Understanding this state of affairs — and such is, most definitely, an affair of the state — occupies so much dinner-table discussion in my community, in my circle, folks like me who enjoy the life of the mind and who look with some perplexity and horror at how the world around them has reared an ugly head, spewing hate, articulating the resentments and fears of a class of people, generally white, generally privileged, who are losing their grip on privilege, slowly, steadily, the world around *them* becoming more complicated, stranger, different. Becoming legion.

In some of my worst moments, I suppose that, as a queer man, I want to welcome them to my world. I want to welcome them to a lifetime of fear. I want to say, "Hail, fellow traveler. Now you are beginning to see what I have seen, feel what I have felt, live a part of what I've lived. You know the fear of walking down a street, wondering when the next assault will come from. Note: I don't say *if* the assault will come, but *when*." Part of me can't help but feel glad that they are starting to feel the fear.

But we're not quite there yet. Their fear is still manifesting as the privilege of acting out, of being able to throw a tantrum, of lashing out because their worlds have been made a little less secure, when in fact most of what's happened is that their world has begun to look a bit different. They probably aren't experiencing any less security than they have for some time (at least not yet, though they will). Instead, for many of them I wager, their fear of change is responding to the more visible presence of different races and nationalities and genders and sexualities. They are not yet ready to become part of the world that many of us are already familiar with, those whose sense of the world was never one of security, who were always waiting for the next attack, the expected violation. Audre Lorde calls us those who "were never meant to survive."[7]

What do you do with such consciousness of oneself, with the awareness that you were never really meant to survive? If this

---

7   From Audre Lorde's amazing poem, "Litany for Survival," one of the first poems in which I felt I recognized myself as a queer person.

book has a goal, an agenda, a thesis, it's in asking this question. *What have I done with such a consciousness? What do I continue to do every day with the violations perpetrated on my body and soul? What can and must I do to survive a life, one that was never meant to survive?*

I walk into this coffee shop, nearly every morning, early, to write these words, to think through the thoughts that crowd my head, the voices, always the voices, the many throbbing voices that have been given to me. I try to calm my mind, sitting with my coffee, sipping quietly, praying that the voices won't overtake me, that they won't drown out the questions that I put to them, the questions that I ask of them.

This is hard enough. And then I notice yet again the group of young men sitting across from me, all in their twenties. All slim, many bearded, different races, all here in the early morning, enjoying one another's company. Southern California hipsters. They laugh, they joke, they talk and seem to share of themselves with one another. I suspect they are all straight, but even so I can see the camaraderie, the pleasure they seem to take in their company, and I'm glad. I wanted such as a young man. I was denied just such as a young man. But I'm glad that it exists, that men can find a way with one another to share a table, to be comfortable with one another. I'm almost too old at this point to envy it. But I can still acknowledge it and think it good, a desirable thing, a thing I want for these men — to be at home with one another in ways that I longed for, but couldn't be, was not allowed to be.

And then they bow their heads and start to pray. What I'm seeing is an early morning prayer group, a group of christians who have come together to fortify themselves for the day, not just through their companionship, but by praying to a god who thought it fit to sacrifice his son, who could see no other way to reconcile himself *to his own creations* than through the terrible torture and death of his only-begotten son.

These may not be the men I think they were. I'm more and more sure these are not the men I thought they were. My lip quivers, my left eye twitches. I can feel the fear deep inside me, pressing out on my flesh. I sit quietly, I can already feel myself trying to make myself invisible. I had been looking, glancing over, thinking of these men. Now I want them not to notice me. I pray to their god that they don't notice me. *Dear lord, please protect me from your followers.* These are the kinds of men who made my youth a living hell. They made for me the kind of life that the believe their god reserves for the most wicked. They practiced what they imagined their god prepares for the outcast and the unclean. They did not set aside a devil for me. They offered me the devil at hand — their contempt, their scorn, their hatred. *Fag, faggot, queer, cocksucker.*

The part of me that is not still a little boy knows that I am being unfair to these men. They have not overtly threatened me. For all I know, their christianity might be, as some christians say, "open and affirming," actually welcoming of people like me. I used to worship in such a church. So, maybe they would welcome me. I don't know. I admit that I will not ask. Oh, I imagine it, imagine asking. I imagine the possible conversation. The academic in me, the idealist academic in me who believes that nearly anything can be talked out, talked through, even possibly understood, thinks that maybe I should try to have that conversation with them. But in the moment, in this particular moment, I'm sitting as still as I can. *Please don't notice me. Please. No, I'm not looking at you, I'm not checking you out, there's nothing to see here.* But of course I was checking them out, I was looking, I was even desiring — if not their flesh then at least their ease, their presumed ease in the world. I'm already guilty. They wouldn't be wrong even if they thought that I thought some of them cute, a couple of them worth more sustained attention. Such is the insidious nature of this dynamic: I am what they might fear, the probing eye that is drawn to them in ways that they might not be drawn to me.

But do I then need to live in fear of that mismatch? Is it necessary that I live in fear of being recognized — and hated?

These may not be the men I think they are. I pray these are not the men I fear, that they are not the men and boys who abused me as a child. I pray that their easy companionship is just that, a security in each other that is more of openness and generosity than the toxic belief that each is just exactly like the other. But I'm not yet convinced. When you bow your heads together and pray to one god, you must imagine that you are praying to just one god, that the boy next to you is praying to the same god. And the act of praying to one god is itself the practice of aligning, the disciplining of collective will toward one end. Maybe not always, but often enough. Thy will be done. *Thy will.*

And *thy will* is what might still animate the boys of Covington Catholic, or the priests and pastors who abuse. Thy will is what suggests to such men, such boys, that the bodies of others, but especially the bodies of others not like them, and most particularly the female and queer and colored, remain permeable to their desires, remain open and even inviting of their contempt, their assault, their moral outrage, their violation. *Thy will be done.*

Our MAGA-capped brothers and sisters may be starting to learn that they too, in the eyes of the rich, are possessed of permeable bodies that they have never quite fully been in possession of. They themselves have already been bought and sold. They are living on the financialized ruins of an economy that can no longer sustain the delusion of their mastery. What's ultimately changed isn't just the more visible presence of people like me, formerly outcast and other, but the steady erosion of white privileged economic security, changed and increasingly destroyed through predatory capitalist practices and the machinations of the rich who have chipped away for decades at pensions, unions, social welfare, and social security. These brothers and sisters are slowly but surely becoming the wretched of the earth.

I wonder, will we — the outcast and other — be able at some point to welcome them? Will we be able to see in them their own humanity, even as they fail to see ours? What traumas, inherited and grotesque, will their generations have to suffer through, just to begin to cleanse the stain of other people's blood on their hands, the hands put to the wheel of empire, the hands looping the rope around a young Black gay man's neck?

***

And now I'm writing this when the news blasts with reports that Jussie Smollett may have paid the two young men to accost and violate him, and in fact he's being arrested for reporting false information to the police. The scene of assault may have been scripted, staged, enacted on purpose. An act concocted by an actor. Smollett remained quiet for a couple of days and then vehemently, painfully denied the counter-accusation. How could he have done such a thing? Who would do such a thing? And then the arrest announcement. It's not looking good for him.

The dynamics of this story astound. The speeds of circulation make the story of the initial assault itself a kind of violation, reports pounding out the awful resonances with lynching. And then, just as quickly, the counter-strike appears because there are so many who just don't want to believe that this sort of thing happens, or they eagerly want to believe that someone like Smollett would stage the attack to score political points for Blacks and gays, perhaps as a career move as well, courting sympathy.

And what gets lost in all of this noise, all of this noise, is the fact that this kind of thing *does* happen, even if it didn't happen to Jussie Smollett. It happens.

But even more, what's not even recognized, not even recognized because it's just too perverse to be seen, much less acknowledged, is that someone like Jussie might grow up, so Black, so gay, so damaged by racism and homophobia that staging such a scene is not inconceivable. That it might be the way to cultivate some attention for all the slights, harms, and violations, great and small, that constitute the life of an other in this culture, abusive and violent. I have to admit that that makes sense to me. I get that. Not everyone will. But I get it, even though I don't know Jussie, and I'm not saying that that's what happened. I have no idea why Jussie Smollett, in this particular time and place, may have fabricated a racist and homophobic assault against his person. Perhaps one day we will know about his particular time and place. But, in the meantime, I can imagine why someone might do such a thing.

I don't condone it. But I get it.

***

PART THREE

Overgrowth

I remember sitting with a colleague, a friend, after I published my first memoir, *Creep,* and had sent him a copy to read. He is a distinguished scholar, well-published, a journalist, even a Pulitzer Prize-winning author. He'd been our neighbor and we'd become friends, and I was really curious about his thoughts on the book — both as an author but also, frankly, as my neighbor, someone who had gotten to know me, if not extremely intimately, at least in a more than passing way, as someone who had seen a bit of my domestic life, as I'd seen a bit of his. We had lunch at a somewhat expensive restaurant in Irvine that he liked, and I was glad to meet him there. After all, I'd asked him to read my book.

Of all the things we talked about, two remain with me to this day. Our friendly and engaging conversation, which I anticipated being as such, ranged over many subjects, but I was struck first — and forcefully — by what he called my "overgrowth." I'd never heard the word before, but it seemed apt to describe the many ways in which I've pursued professional and cultural accomplishment in light of (to compensate for?) my significantly more humble working-class beginnings in south Louisiana. Overgrowth captures something that's not just fecund and fertile but perhaps dangerously so. It threatens to crowd out other forms of life, one aspect of an ecology overtaking another. And aren't we, after all, ecologies, systems we imagine unto ourselves but also in deep relationship with neighboring ecologies and networks? I think my colleague meant to congratulate me on what he perceived as a phenomenal act of overcoming, perhaps even overachieving, though I don't in any way feel like an overachiever. But the darker resonances of overgrowth struck me then and have stayed with me.

What life am I crowding out? What aspects of my being languish or remain underdeveloped — or have actually *died* — because I couldn't or didn't attend to them while I was focusing on building myself professionally, cultivating defensively the kind of life of security and moderate prosperity that would signal that there's nothing damaged here, there's only the good stuff, success, value, pride in a job well done?

What my friend didn't know is that I've been compensating for a long time, not just for my humble beginnings but for the many ways in which my childhood was violated, abused, and consequently denied me. Someone else might have insisted on having the childhood they never got to have, acting out as a juvenile, taking unnecessary risks, being like a kid. I've taken another route, falling into what some gay therapists have labeled the "best little boy in the world" syndrome. I couldn't be the star athlete, or the most popular smart kid. I wasn't going to be an average and likable Joe. But I could be studious, dedicated, nerdy, and successful. *Revenge of the Nerds* after all was a movie playing during my senior year in high school. I absorbed the lesson. I would rise to victory yet. We are the champions of the world. Or at least I could aim for a certain kind of professional championship. I finished my PhD at twenty-five. I earned tenure in my early thirties. I became a full professor before forty. I started my own gay family, with or without kids, a decision kicked down the road, but still a family of my own. I'm not wealthy, but I'm published and respected. I've even try my hand at administration, building programs, starting centers, hiring and firing and raising money and doing all the things that administrators do.

I've done all of this and have found it actually fairly satisfying. Not completely — no, nothing, no one *thing* can ever be *completely* satisfying. But I've done a good job, I've done it ahead of schedule, I've been, if not the *best* little boy in the world, at least a very very *good boy,* and I've shown that I wasn't someone who should've been harassed, tormented, abused, victimized. I didn't deserve it. It wasn't me. It wasn't what I wanted, after all. I didn't ask for it. It was a mistake. No, it was a *crime.* It was criminal what was done to me, and criminal for the teachers and priests and pastors to fail to recognize — fuck, to actually ignore at times what was happening to me, to become complicit in their ignoring. My pain was *their* personal failure. It still *is* to this day *their* personal — and professional and ethical and moral — *failure.* They *failed me.* And I've had to bolster myself, raise myself up in ways they couldn't, overcome *their failure* to prove that it wasn't me, I didn't ask for it. I didn't deserve it.

None of this my distinguished friend could really focus on. And perhaps that was my failure, and why I'm writing this new book. Indeed, in writing *Creep* I certainly described the bullying I suffered, and I mentioned my uncle, and I gestured to the possibility that he might have sort of abused me, maybe. But in identifying myself as a creep, in focusing attention on my internalized sense of my own creepiness, my own oddity and weirdness, and *not* turning as much attention to the fact that there was something to be internalized that *wasn't* originally a part of me — homophobic abuse — I was taking the blame, I was owning my creepiness, I was laying claim to the kinds of desires that, thankfully, I know better (mostly) than to foist on other people. At least I hope so.

And this is another kind of overgrowth, this constant questioning, this continual self-examination, this predisposition given to me to monitor myself ceaselessly, to probe and when necessary puncture my own delusions, question my desires, force my own hand to own up to my own bullshit. What does this look like? It might vary from day to day, but some patterns are consistent. I have notebooks, journals, lists on my phone that are quite literally lists of things that I'm worrying about, that cause anxiety, items onto which my mind has glommed to fixate, fondle, probe for the rotting bit that will poison the totality of my life. I nurse these lists, visiting them daily, crossing out items, adding others. Is that ping I heard in the car the initial warning sign of automotive catastrophe? Is that lukewarm handshake the beginning of the end of an otherwise collegial professional relationship? Will we be audited? How might my graduate student's fumbling attempts on the job market ultimately circle back to reflect, indeed magnify my supreme incompetence at my job, my total lack of fitness for my tenured full professorship?

As you can see, much of this isn't necessarily stuff that will amount to much. Or if any individual item amounts to anything, it's usually a sum that's bearable, fully manageable. More perversely, I've often understood my anxiety disorder — for disorder it is: how much precious time wasted in agony, pacing in my room, self-medicating with a midday cocktail, trying to calm myself from the fallout of the fevered fantasy of impending and imminent doom, the ping in the car becoming the crash that kills a pedestrian and results in my inevitable incarceration for vehicular manslaughter — yes, I've tried at times to understand this anxiety disorder as a coping mechanism gone slightly awry, but with a kernel of something good buried, however deeply, still there.

Psychoanalytic theorist Karen Horney described neuroses as defense mechanisms that have become pathological, our natural and necessary defenses turned against us (we live, after all, in a world that, if it isn't exactly out to get us, is at least not always supporting our growth, maturation, and well-being, much less happiness). It's appropriate for me to be monitoring my social and professional networks, for instance; that's an understandable proactive defensiveness. But when I spend an afternoon sipping my vodka cocktail in an attempt to reduce my anxiety-induced fit over how an otherwise friendly colleague's greeting today was less than enthusiastic than I hoped it would be, then yes, I have a disorder. Something's wrong. *Nurse the network, but excise the fear,* I tell myself. Again and again. And then I write it down in a list, tracking my feeling of this anxiety, noting how the next day the colleague seems to be OK and I can, thank god, cross this worry off my list.

It's too soon replaced by another. If there's anything I can truly trust in this world, it is my mind's capacity to find the next available anxiety.

What I'm encountering here in rehearsing this accounting of my anxiety, and inviting you to encounter in the process, is the sense of my own *twisting*, the many ways in which whatever happened to me, I've been winding my way around it for a very long time. And the way is admittedly convoluted. It is, to be fair, *many* ways, not just one. It has become multiple paths that I follow at any given moment, on any given day, to tell this story, to narrate a life, to make sense of my becoming.

This too is overgrowth. It's a weedful life, flourishing with a muchness, but also a madness.

So now a different question, but related, intimately, one I find myself avoiding but also needing to return to: what has this overgrowth cost me? What is this overgrowth crowding out? For the compensation combined with the constant vigilance is at times, quite frankly, my dear reader, exhausting. And I worry (another item for the list!) that I'm missing out on something.

Curiously, my friend, the colleague I'm sitting with in this fancy restaurant, provides a possible answer in the other item upon which he comments, a notable lack that he identifies in my writing. For a queer memoirist, a gay life-writer, I don't comment that much on my sex life. Most of the gay writers he's read, in particular Edmund White, that master of autofiction, spend a great deal of time talking about their sex lives, the moment of their first sexual encounter with a member of the same sex becoming just the first in a series of often lurid and detailed descriptions of man-on-man fucking. He's not wrong, about either the propensity of gay male memoir to forefront the sexual, even the nastily sexual, and my own avoidance of it in much of my writing about myself. (I suspect this book will not be much different, but we will see. I'm already second guessing myself.)

We can elucidate reasons for this propensity in queer, and specifically gay male, memoir. When your sexuality has been proscribed and made pathological to yourself and toxic to the larger culture, then naturally, once you discover it is not so, and indeed once you realize that approaching and getting the sexual intimacy that you've longed for is not only *not* bad for you but the very thing that in many cases will save your life and make it worth living — well, no wonder that many gay men understand the description of their erotic lives as not only personally necessary but politically powerful. Such narratives become one of the primary ways in which queers offer a counter-narrative to the rest of the world. *See, fuckers? This sex isn't killing me. It's saving my life. It's giving me joy and pleasure and possibility you can't know because you're stuck in your cookie-cutter worlds, fucking in ways you were told you should, loving in your limited and pathetically pre-invented lives. I'd say "fuck you" but I don't want to. You'd only bring me down.*

Well, there are many versions of this story, including the one in which saying that this love isn't killing me is, alas, not exactly true for some people in the late 20th century. If anything, though, AIDS provided yet another opportunity to fight the narrative that queer sex is bad bad bad. And I love writers like Edmund White who have fought that fight, who write the wrongs of our supposedly tainted love.

I don't know that I'm one of those writers. I have avoided explicit description of my own sexual experiences, for the most part. I don't kiss and tell. (I want to tell you that as I was typing out "kiss" I actually was typing out "kill" but that might just be too precious.). I think I am going to correct that in this book, at least partially, if only because I understand that it's a thing that needs a kind of correction. I've been avoiding again, not telling, not showing the thing that perhaps I should be telling.

In another way, though, my friend was wrong. I have been writing about my sexual experiences all along. He just didn't see it. He couldn't spot it because it doesn't look like Edmund White's kind of sexual story. It's not the usual narrative.

I've been writing about my abuse my entire life. And I'm only realizing it now myself.

And that's why it will take a while to get to sex as pleasure, my body as anything other than the vehicle of potential terror.

***

While I absolutely understand how the cycles and economics of drug addiction and circulation are products of complex social relations, I also understand drug use as a deeply personal affair. I'm writing this at a time of increasing liberality around marijuana, at least in some parts of the US. My current home state, California, is one of a handful that has legalized pot for recreational use. I think that's a good thing. At the same time, news of the opioid crisis continues to reveal the extent to which opioids were over-prescribed, abused by patients who became addicted to them but in turn profitable for the companies that made them. Manufacturers would push doctors to dole out opiates on their patients, the patients not fully understanding the dangers of the drugs and some of the doctors getting kickbacks for prescribing them. I experienced the power of opioids firsthand, having gone to my endodontist for a double root canal and walking out of his office with a prescription for thirty hydrocodone. I didn't need that many. I'm not sure I needed any at all. If the dentist performed his surgery correctly, then I wouldn't be feeling anything in the leftover shells of those teeth. But I took one that evening and I won't deny it — it blissed me out. I experienced a profound body high. I lay in my bed, my body becoming increasingly numb, but my mind fully aware of what was going on around me. I picked up a book and read for hours, late into the night, while my body lay supine and prone, content and pleased. I loved it.

I began parsing out the pills, cutting them in half, using them only on Fridays, at the end of the week, wanting a bit of relaxation. I'd take half a hydrocodone and get into bed to read. It was heaven. I ran out of the pills in time, but friends would give me theirs, knowing how much I adored the feeling of my body, numbed, sedated, but my mind able to sink into a book. Such a good Friday night. Some of the best Friday nights I've had.

No, I'm not addicted to opiates. But I totally understand how someone could be. These aren't intoxicating, at least not in the dosages that I consumed. But the peace and tranquility were completely captivating to me. I don't wonder about why. If you have a sufficiently complex relationship to your body — and I certainly do, my more intense sexual experiences being about inflicting pain on my body — then a drug that removes you from your body, that numbs it, will also have its attractions. There's no contradiction here. I'm either punishing my body or I'm trying to get away from it. It's the same predisposition, just approached from slightly different angles. I hate my body. It's a constant reminder of my vulnerability, my penetrability. So I'm either going to control how much pain it can receive, or I'm going to eliminate its ability to register any breach.

If I weren't more stable — emotionally, financially, professionally — I'd likely pursue the kind of experience afforded by hydrocodone all the time. I might even advance further in my exploration of opiates as the effects of one particular drug began to lessen. I'd likely alternate between intense punishment of my body, seeking out increasingly damaging sessions of torture on one hand, forcing my body for instance through a grueling workout at the gym, and rotating such pain with extended periods of blissed-out numbness on the other. I get that, totally. It is within reason, the unreason of addiction, the cycle that keeps the body at bay, that renders your somatic demon sated and pacified.

I'm not fully there. I'll likely never be there. But I have significant empathy for those who fall into similar kinds of cycles. Admittedly theirs are not going to look just like mine, but I understand the dynamic here, I think. Lauren Berlant might call this a version of "slow death," the kind of practice of perverse self-care (although I don't think she uses that word) that offers a bit of relief, even a bit of pleasure in the moment, but that actually is killing you in the long haul. Think of the pleasures of fast food, for instance. The grease, the salt, the juicy burger (that's made of meat products that have to be fortified with protein powder in order for them to qualify federally as "meat") — something convenient, something fast, something pleasurable, something that you might turn to, might even have to turn to, at the end of the day because you're just too tired from having worked at your back-breaking job for the last ten or so hours. You eat it, it feels good in your mouth, it fills your belly. It's also slowly killing you.

And then at night, you pop an opiate with a glass of cheap whiskey and go to bed with the television chattering at you. You're literally surrounded by poisons, ingesting them, hearing them, seeing them, sleeping with them.

Why does a life of privilege start to seem now like all of the attempts at one's disposal to fend off slow death? Maybe that's not what a life of privilege is "like"; that's what a life of privilege *actually is.*

But still, there's a deus ex opioid for someone like me, the temptation, the realization that I can numb myself when I need to. My other privileged friends will supply me with their pills. We pass them around like candy, eyeing the gleam in each other's eyes as we gaze on the gifts of sedation. Our death is just a bit slower than that of those down the road, working paycheck to paycheck, but it still feels like death — numbing the anxieties, those nagging neurotic tics and thoughts that accumulate over the course of the day or as the return of the repressed from past trauma.

I keep telling myself there is no reason to feel bad. Things are going well. But there *are* reasons. There are reasons that have to do with my own particular personal experience, surely. But there are reasons too that are structural, that are about longer and systemic histories of bigotry against queer people, of the toxic training men go through in the codes and repressions of masculinity, of the fact for instance that I'm the only out gay man in my English department, that I made it this far but that in this particular case I am also still anomalous, that I'm the one they let in, that even now in a more and more tolerant age *we can only let in just so many people like you.* But still, I keep telling myself that there is no reason to feel bad.

I have at times throughout my life attempted various psycho-pharmacological interventions. Right around the time of my divorce, then again when my father died, I sought out psychiatrists who might prescribe some intermingling of talk therapy and medication. Prozac left my dick lifeless, but Welbutrin didn't. I took them to get me through the dissolution of my marriage. Lexapro saw me through my father's death. To be sure,

I'm not sure that any of these medicines "got me through," but they accompanied me, with odd effects. Besides Prozac's deadening effects on my cock, Lexapro had the next most noticeable side-effects. I'd be walking along in a mall, perhaps stopping at a Starbucks, and then all of a sudden everything would be intensely bright and pleasant for just a split second, as though I'd run through a minor overflow of joy seeping through from some heavenly realm or dimension of paradise. But only a split second. Otherwise, I just grieved throughout the day, numb.

More recently, though, thinking that enough is enough, that I'm tired of waking up in the middle of the night, wondering if I'm going to be fired from my job because I forgot to do some nearly meaningless bureaucratic task, checking the door in the middle of the night to make sure that it's locked so that we aren't assaulted and killed, feeling intensely the slights of colleagues who didn't say hello but who really just didn't see me as they are so wrapped up in their own worlds, their own anxieties — thinking *enough is enough,* I consulted with a local psychiatrist whom a friend recommended, saying that he's essentially a pill pusher, someone who won't want to talk, who will just offer you medication in the belief that pretty much every psychological ailment has a physiological cause and cure.

I remember being in the waiting room before my appointment, the place perhaps a bit less nice than I'd hoped. There's a cute hipster across from me, clearly anxious. What's he in here for? Probably like me, some non-debilitating malfunction that's just annoying enough to make you feel like shit. Then there's the middle-aged woman apologizing to the room for the traffic having held her up, making her late, talking to herself as she fills out forms. I start to fill out my own forms, a surprisingly large check-list of physical and psychological issues that I need to confess. *Is my sleep disturbed? Do I have any allergies? Do I want to kill myself?* Yes, no, sort of. I'd already been warned by my friend to be careful in answering the survey. *Remember,* she offered: *this guy can have you committed.* I wasn't too worried, but exercised caution nonetheless.

The hipster is called in and I avert my eyes, offering if not solitude then at least some modicum of false privacy. Curiously there's some classical music playing, and I can't help but tune in, drifting from the form. It's nothing soothing though, but something frenetic, crazily spinning violins and hysterically chuckling brass. I think it's Stravinsky, something plaintively Russian at times. *Firebird*? The hipster emerges moments later and flees. Probably just a refill? Then the receptionist is running after the hipster, and I start to wonder: *what am I doing here?* To be fair to myself, I'd already been wondering that. I think it's sane to wonder what you're doing, what you're really doing, in these kinds of situations. *Do I really want this medication? Why can't I just take care of this on my own? Is drinking myself numb every afternoon really that bad? Many people do that, don't they?*

I know my colleagues and friends have sat on this room. And I know that I'm here in part because not only did one friend recommend this particular psychiatrist, but another friend told me that pretty much everyone I know, everyone I work with, is on some kind of medication. I suspect he's right. But can't I be different? Apparently not. I'm waiting for them to walk in, someone I know, a colleague, a work friend, a friend — but someone I haven't talked to about coming here. And then we would become secret sharers. Would we talk? Acknowledge one another at least? Or avoid contact? Do I know that fleeing hipster? Have I seen him on campus, a graduate student perhaps?

Talking woman goes in, and then comes out. There's a revolving door, a conveyor belt. The music ends and I strain to listen to the voices of the receptionist, the therapist, the clients, trying to catch a name. Is there anyone here I know? The doctor wants to see someone three days a week. I don't want to see anyone three days a week. Weirdly enough this scene is starting to remind me of the time I went with a friend to get a medical marijuana license. This was before recreational marijuana hit California, but who was fooling whom? The waiting room to see the "doctor" (although we were assured he was an actual doctor, a real-life medical doctor) was full of the most stereotypical potheads you can imagine. I kid you not. My friend and

I, college professors in our designer jeans and designer t-shirts, were so completely out of place. The room reeked of pot. No one was smoking it, but it clung to the clothes of those around us. Everyone was bleary-eyed, a bit sedated. They also seemed predominantly from the working class — working-man jeans, torn t-shirts, ragged purses, stains and dirt patches. I couldn't help but think of slow death, people self-medicating, now legally with marijuana, to survive their days, surviving through sedation. And as though on cue the kid next to me asks if we'd been here before. He's a student at a community college down the road and really needs to renew his license before he gets too much further into this chemistry class. It helps with the anxiety. He's got his story down. My friend and I are here just for kicks, but we have prepared our stories: some headaches from tight jaws, back pain, stress.

And indeed, a few years later in a different waiting room, I am rehearsing my comments, preparing my remarks. No, I think I'm really fine, I'm just anxious all the time. I don't sleep well. I check the knob of the front door before I go to bed several times, checking it, rattling it, then walking away, and then walking back, rattling it again, probably four or five, maybe some nights six times. When I wake up in the middle of the night to pee, I check it again, and again. One time, when we had a regular coffeemaker, one of the old kind that wouldn't turn itself off on its own, I turned it off before I went to work, then halfway on my drive to campus, I found myself turning around to go back to the apartment in order to make sure that it was off, starting to cry on the way back home because I knew that it was already off but that I was still going to drive back home to check it. That's a pathology. It's not debilitating; I'm never late for work, I am productive, I do what needs to be done. *I'm overgrown, goddammit!* But something's wrong, I know it's wrong, it makes me sad. Please make it stop.

I tell these stories, and the doctor, an older man who has had some plastic surgery, nods along — *Seems like a garden variety obsessive compulsive disorder, anxiety, seen it before. Nothing to*

*worry about. We can make this stop. Here's your prescription.
Come back in a few months.*

He gives me Klonopin, which is so strange because I'd just heard Bret Easton Ellis, the novelist, talking about it on his podcast. I can't remember if he said he'd taken it himself, but I imagine if he or others in his group did, it was likely the least toxic thing they were taking. I'm a little concerned nonetheless. Isn't this what mid-century housewives took when they couldn't quite manage the ceaseless rounds of dishwashing, clothes washing, packing lunches, making welcome-home cocktails for their returning husbands? Mommy's little helper? Am I that person now? I thought that, in coming here, I was actually doing something good for myself, helping to stabilize myself. I'd even talked myself into thinking that I was engaging in the *art of living*, not just surviving, but rather taking advantage of medical advancements to fine-tune my body and mind into more optimal performance.

I think I was wrong. I think I have been deluding myself.

Part of the delusion lies in thinking that the office trappings will make a difference, that this is decidedly different from the time I went with my friend to get a medical marijuana license. But is it? With that said I want to be clear: I think these medicines do actually help many people. I know they help some of my friends, some colleagues, people I've cared about — hell, even people I don't particularly like. I have read about these interventions, I attempt to be informed. I read *Prozac Nation* and *Listening to Prozac* as I took my first fluoxetine hydrochloride pills, trying to listen to my own body, my own mind as the chemicals worked over the synapses in my brain.

But I begin to wonder, my mind and body spinning out on the drugs, smoking some pot, jiving on a hydrocodone. *What are we doing? What are we really doing?* Aldous Huxley in *The Doors of Perception* wants to make experimentation with "some chemical Door in the Wall" (he chose mescaline) a part of formal education. *We should expand our minds, we should expand*

our children's minds, our survival as a species might depend on it.[1]
Then the Brat Pack authors I grew up reading, Bret Easton Ellis
and Jay McInerney, wrote characters who extolled the various
virtues of cocaine, the magically enabling substance that fueled
marathon work sessions and then marathon party sessions,
work, party, work, party. Then smoking pot with my friends
on various trips out to Colorado and Oregon, where marijuana
has been increasingly not just legalized but culturally main-
streamed. Walking into a pot store in Portland, asking the kid at
the counter to "make me happy" and the kid showing me a glass
case full of various kinds of chemically induced forms of happiness, a jewel case, gold-and-diamond-studded happiness just
waiting to be ingested. Then walking outside, the pot cushion-
ing our stroll through the cloudy city, floating on a cloud, and
then I'm walking through five seconds of sheer bliss, sheer un-
adulterated joy — *five seconds of bliss,* I tell you. And then more
floating, floating, floating. Later that night, coming down off the
high, I lay in bed with my laptop open, playing a new episode of
Shameless, that story of lower-class intoxication and addiction,
centered on an alcoholic and abusive father, a son drugged up
to numb the pain of his misunderstood brilliance, a dedicated
but misguided daughter trying to keep everything together. But
what is *everything*? Why must we keep everything together? Isn't
the point of all of this, all of these drugs, the mind expansion,
the coke-fueled partying, the alcoholic numbing, the deadening
Klonopins — isn't the goal to let go, let go, let it all go?

But no, no, can't go there. Not totally, not today, maybe not
ever. In *Shameless,* after all, the father, Frank, is hardly a reliable
apologist for the joys of turning away from any kind of social
or personal responsibility; he's a total fucking selfish shit. And
one mistake with cocaine comes close to destroying Fiona's, the
responsible daughter's, life, as she is caught with it while preg-

---

1   Even today, Huxley's little book makes for some compelling reading. It was
    originally published in 1954. Compare it to Michael Pollan's more recent
    *How to Change Your Mind: What the New Science of Psychedelics Teaches
    Us About Consciousness, Dying, Addiction, Depression, and Transcendence,*
    published in 2018.

nant; we viewers are then treated to the gruesome spectacle of the crack baby — this is what drugs birth, this and this *predominantly.* You can't escape; you're only ever temporarily numbed, reality coming back with a vengeance. And then another favorite show, *Nurse Jackie,* the incredible Edie Falco, moved on from the mafioso family of *The Sopranos* to her own working-class neighborhood, job, family, and life, stealing opioids and faking prescriptions just to cope with day-to-day survival. And then the chemistry teacher in *Breaking Bad* trying to lessen the pain of his cancer and provide a nest egg for his family given his the death sentence of his illness. No, there's nothing about mind expansion, about partying, about *bliss, about walking through five seconds of bliss* here. This is all about coping. There is nothing in *Shameless, Nurse Jackie,* or *Breaking Bad* that romances drugs. If anything, in *Breaking Bad,* Heisenberg resorts to making drugs so that he can provide for his financially tenuous family and then seems psychopathically engaged in the pursuit of success — which itself might be a critique of neoliberal capitalism: the product doesn't matter, but the success of it at any cost does. Similarly, *Nurse Jackie* seems to use opioids just in order to get through the day and succeed as a nurse. We know nothing of her backstory, and her addiction is just categorized as addiction — and yet the constant reminders that she is an excellent nurse and needs the opioids to help her cope is itself a critique of contemporary work cultures.

These are shows about managing one's relationship to pain. In fact, I'll go so far as to say these shows aren't even about particular drugs or even really about addiction, which I understand as a very real problem for those afflicted with it. They are instead about the need to cope, the need to find some spaces that are free of grinding physical and psychic pain. They are not about joy. They are not about bliss. They are not about mind expansion. We as a culture are not telling ourselves stories about hippie drugs. We are telling ourselves stories about drugs that help get one through an awful day — and that the drugs you give yourself will kill you but that the drugs you might get from a psychiatrist, if you can afford one, probably won't. These are lessons in appropriate and licensed forms of coping. But the overriding message is clear: we desperately need ways to cope. We can't do this on our own. The larger culture, a capitalist culture, positions us primarily as subjects in need of a fix.

In the week immediately following the election of Donald Trump, I took a Klonopin every night before going to bed. I needed to cope. I needed to fix something in me because I couldn't fix something in the bigger world. I still need to cope, but I know too that my problems run deeper than Donald Trump, though it's nice to have a sign, such an immensely visible sign, of everything that's wrong with the world.

And yet, I still want joy. I want not just to cope. I want to be free of the obsessive-compulsive need to check every lock, to make sure the coffee pot is turned off, and turned off, checking again and checking again and again. I want the five seconds of bliss, just walking through five seconds of bliss. I want not to be violated by the ceaseless media that positions medication as coping, that offers drugs as various forms of better or worse coping. I am working on it. I am working on the balance here, even as I don't want the balance anymore. I just want joy.

I leave the psychiatrist's office with my prescription, get to my car, and google the radio station playing in his waiting room. I want to know what that music was.

It is *Firebird*. I am so relieved.

***

Thinking about drugs and drug use that stems from abuse, the television adaptation of Edward St. Aubyn's Patrick Melrose novels is, for me at least, fortuitous. I had not heard of these books, didn't know of their existence (or if I did, they didn't penetrate my consciousness sufficiently to note them) until I came across them in a bookstore in Wellington, New Zealand, while I was wandering around between visits with friends. I took a picture of the cover of the omnibus edition and queued it up on Amazon, where the item lingered (as most of my queued items tend to linger) for a half-year until I heard about the television adaptation, starring Benedict Cumberbatch. I bought the books and started reading — and I have to admit that they are pretty stunning. The series starts off as a very Evelyn-Waugh type send-up of the British upper class. The narrator is largely snide, with some philosophical wisdom about the corruption of class thrown in periodically to remind you, à la Waugh, that a satirist is also a moralist. I had been thinking about going back to Waugh, re-reading *Brideshead Revisited,* that super-important book of my youth — but I dived instead into St. Aubyn's Melrose family saga, tempted far less by the class critique and more by the novels' personally immediate story: the son Patrick's abuse by his father.[2]

As abuse goes, it's spectacular abuse. Not only is David Melrose viciously unkind and psychologically cutting, he also sexually abuses his son between the ages of five and eight, at which point Patrick has had enough and can start to fight back. If you didn't know the abuse was coming, it would totally take you by surprise. You'd experience it as a violation. The first two-thirds of the first novel, *Never Mind,* pivots around the petty and awful behavior of a group of landed and would-be aristocrats; the jockeying and put-downs build until you, as a reader, want out. And then the scene: David, punishing Patrick for miscellaneous

---

2   *Never Mind, Bad News, Some Hope, Mother's Milk,* and *At Last* comprise the Patrick Melrose Novels, published individually between 1992 and 2012. They are semi-autobiographical. The five-part dramatic miniseries, tracking each novel individually, appeared in 2018 and was distributed in the US by Showtime.

and unclear offenses, but mostly just wanting to exert his control over another body, throws his son on the bed and jerks off over his prone and motionless form. The scene creeps up on you and then its horror delivers a punch when St. Aubyn's narrator describes Patrick feeling his father's semen slinking down between his butt cheeks. (I'm writing this from memory. I'm not going to quote the passage — in part because you should read it for yourself, but also because I'm interested, as a reader interested in abuse narratives, to see if I have recalled this scene accurately. At this point in my book, I think you know the drill.). This initial violation happens quickly, and we only learn well into the third book, *Some Hope,* that it happened again, or something like it happened again, and again, for three or so years. It's only well into that third book that Patrick sits with one of his best and oldest friends to tell him of the abuse. But it's clear that this sexual assault has shaped Patrick's life irrevocably: it is the primary — and primal — scene that he will have to contend with, grapple with, suffer with, and ultimately live with, if he is to live at all.

These are novels, made up and concocted. Designed and planned. And this narrative arc — the primal scene of abuse, somewhere a child is being fucked by his father — is obviously chosen and worked over, the characters involved in this domestic tragedy laboring under it. St. Aubyn chooses to make the abuse central, in part by making everything else in the novels so shallow, so relentlessly shallow. The other characters are generally deplorable. They are vapid social climbers, or ciphers who do whatever they can to maintain their hold on class status. Many are likely alcoholics, numbing themselves through days of veiled insults, slights, and threats at parties that few if any of them really want to attend. Patrick is perhaps the worst of the lot, so suffice it to say that he's not a shining example or moral compass or ethical star by which one might guide oneself into, through, and out of a set of people whom you really wouldn't want to spend much time with — unless you're the kind of vapid individual who desperately wants to be one of them. (And if you are, good luck to you.) No, Patrick becomes the center of the novels because of the bit of awfulness and horror he suffers at the hands of his father, this true sin, this terrible violation; everything else just whirls and twirls around it.

As does Patrick, who seems just to stumble through much of his life until middle age when some kind of "peace" is attained. Before then, we see him in the grisly second novel — appropriately titled *Bad News* — fall headlong into chronic drug use, on a merry-go-ground cycle of cocaine and heroin, cocaine and heroin, ramping up his psyche and body and then numbing them before the inevitable heart attack and collapse. *Bad News,* barely more than a hundred pages, is difficult but compelling reading as we watch Patrick deep-dive into escape, a flight prompted by the death of his father on a trip to New York and Patrick's own trip to fetch his remains. I had to laugh out loud while reading this tough material when Patrick sits alone in his swank Manhattan hotel, getting high, his father's ashes in a box and Patrick wondering if he should flush the dust down the toilet. (Given how distant, how emotionally neglectful my father was, I've had the same thought myself about his remains. I might still send them on their way to the California sewers once my mother passes. I'm not sure. And neither is Patrick, who doesn't do it; perhaps that would be just too much, pushing him beyond the pale of readerly identification. But I wouldn't have minded.)

Eventually, Patrick has to return to Europe to grapple with what has happened to him, the fearful legacy his father left him. And this is the narrative arc toward which these novels bend. At one point, nearly in the middle of the omnibus, in the middle of the third novel, the narrator asks, "What was the thread that held together the scattered beads of experience if not the pressure of interpretation?" We are supposedly hearing Patrick's thoughts, but this question likely stands in for the project of the novels, for their reason for being, for the reason many people read them: the question bears within it the assertion that what we are, what we experience, all of our varied encounters, feelings, thoughts, and actions, are so many bits and pieces that would be fragmentary, disconnected, and meaningless unless they are made to *make* sense because of an interpretive imperative. The *will* to meaningfulness accompanies the wills to power and knowledge. St. Aubyn might here be collapsing the will to power and the will to knowledge into the will to make meaning — for making meaning is often an act of tremendous force, the imposition of knowledge through power, the telling of the story the way you want it to be told. Indeed, the very next line, the assertion following this primal question is, "The meaning of life was whatever meaning one could thrust down its reluctant throat." That is, the making of meaning is tantamount to a violation, a fucking of the mouth that is very likely otherwise just spewing nonsense.

Knowledge and violation. The two can't be disentangled from one another in this novel. Patrick's abuse offers him the opportunity, likely the only opportunity offered in these novels, to try to make sense of himself and his world — actually, it is a *demand* to make sense, to salvage something. Nothing else in the books can quite approach a comparable invitation; everything else is petty nonsense, social climbing, selfish viciousness. Another way to read this, of course, is that the abuse might obliterate all other signs and symbols, making a waste of any other semiotics of sense. It thus becomes the experience that Patrick must work with to reconnect himself to the rest of the world. Such is perhaps the narrative arc of many other kinds of narratives of abuse, even those that view the world more generously and charitably than St. Aubyn might; the world is full and plenty and ultimately good, but you have to survive the awfully aberrant thing done to you. I think, though, that the Patrick Melrose novels, given the profoundly vapid lives of everyone surrounding Patrick, can't quite envision that world of plenty and good, and, in the absence of such, the sexual violation perversely becomes the thing that initiates an interpretive imperative, the will to know what happened and why and how one might survive that terrible knowledge. As the drug addiction depicted in *Bad News* suggests, though, that imperative might kill you first. There's so much to fix.

I admire the dedication of these books to their cause, to stripping away of all supports and potential crutches so we can ultimately focus our attention on the devastation of sexual abuse. I wish my own story were as simple. My own drug use, my own attempts at flight, my youthful sexual adventures in sadomasochism (more on this in a bit), my deep dive into escapist reading: none of these are as spectacular as Patrick's — spectacular, a word I used earlier to describe the primal scene. But this scene is in a set of novels that, by definition, must be spectacular, offering scene upon scene to captivate and propel interest, even if through disgust and morbid curiosity, so you can eventually — and self-satisfyingly — reach the end over 800 pages later. Dedication, I tell you, to get through all of that.

But what happens when the scene, the originating scene, is lost, or perhaps less than primal, or more diffused through a set of social relations that position you as always already outcast, thrust to the margins? What if the abuse, the violation, isn't particular, localized, chronologically contained in a chronic form — but part of the formlessness of your existence itself? Still, I sense a connection, my own connection here to Patrick and St. Aubyn's understanding of abuse, to how it becomes everything. And maybe that's what I take away from these books: the violation is everything, no matter its precise form. It becomes everything, inescapable.

Is this our interpretive imperative, the pressure to make meaning? Is this the lesson we keep thrusting down our throats, the lesson I keep fucking myself with, again and again?

***

And now for something completely different. Or not.

I admit that I'm fascinated by the body of Deadpool, the Marvel "superhero" or anti-hero, but really someone who is more of a completely morally compromised mercenary and whose particular mutant ability is that he, like the more nuanced and brooding Wolverine, can regenerate pretty much any part of his body after it's been maimed, cut, punctured, beaten, severed, or otherwise violated. As such, he's nearly indestructible. But unlike Wolverine, who simmers with rage about his condition, Deadpool seems to delight in his body's ability to suffer punishment and rebound, grow back, regenerate. In the comics, he's a pretty minor character, on the periphery of a lot of major narrative action, and he's known mostly for circling the fringes of society and deploying his abilities for his own gain. He can rip off the bad guys ripping off other people and get away with it, that severed arm growing back in due time.

In the movies about Deadpool (of which there are at two as of this writing, with a third in the works), he's played with great slapstick by Ryan Reynolds, and we get more of a sense of his backstory, more character development, and more of a glimpse into his (possible) moral core.[3] His origin story links him to a pretty villainous group that turns the desperate and down on their luck into obedient slaves. Deadpool, before he's Deadpool with his mutant abilities, is just a mercenary, basically a bit of muscle, his regenerative abilities not yet manifesting. He's then diagnosed with a terminal illness, and, with no real access to healthcare (this film being produced at the height of the Obamacare debates), he turns to some truly shady characters who might be able to save his life even if they will then own it. There's a weird story here about healthcare, or at least a pandering to audiences who might themselves be worrying about affordable care. And indeed, references to strained economies and personal finances abound in this film. We learn that Deadpool's name

---

3   *Deadpool* and *Deadpool 2*, released respectively in 2016 and 2018, were distributed by 20th Century Fox, based of course on the Marvel character, as noted.

comes from a wager board that tracks when people are going to die as fodder for placing bets – making the precarity of life itself something that, for some classes of people at least, is subject to a brutal form of financial speculation. Augmenting such uncertainty, the film is self-consciously low, or lower, budget, with not nearly as much money spent on it as the far bigger budget *X-Men* films — a point that Deadpool himself actually mentions during the film, noting how the studio didn't spend money on any major (and expensive) guest appearances from the more mainstream films. Indeed, *Deadpool* is decidedly less "mainstream" than the big-budget films, and it doesn't appeal to everyone. My personal trainer couldn't wait to see *Batman versus Superman,* which I just refused to see, knowing there are only so many hours in the day, in my life; but I couldn't convince him to go see *Deadpool*. It was just too fringe for him, even as much as he claims to love, love, love superhero films.

And I can understand why he would hesitate. Deadpool, both the films and the character, is edgy, atypical, and even somewhat incoherent cartoon fare. The character rants about the injustices of the world, especially those committed against him, but he doesn't necessarily operate with any discernible moral code. He's a mercenary but also struggles to find his heart. He's cocky and arrogant, as one might expect if one can regrow nearly any part of one's body, but he's also capable of sympathetic feeling, perhaps even of love.

But more than these ambiguous qualities, which really extend a cartoonish character into existential territory, Deadpool's body is *disturbing,* and the films seem to relish the presentation of his flesh variously assaulted and regenerating. The opening scene of the first film is a cornucopia of somatic violation. The plot is irrelevant. What's at stake is making sure that you understand that Deadpool can be shot many many times, that he can lose limbs, that his body can be punctured and penetrated — and he'll still survive. He even takes a bullet up his ass, and the character laughs it off as just a shot "right up Main Street." Everyone talks about Deadpool's mouth, his arrogant, snarky, and ceaseless commentary on the world around him; in the comics, he's called the "merc with a mouth." But it's really Deadpool's body that is fascinating, that holds attention, that is the subject not just of much comedic attention in the film but that also drives the plot — in painful and distressing ways.

When Deadpool (before his mutant abilities are revealed) signs his wasting and wasted life over to the villains, thinking they can find a way to save his body, he doesn't realize that what he's signed up for is a grisly round of torture, in which the villains think he's likely a not-yet-realized mutant and are trying to stress his body to the point where his mutant abilities emerge. Once they force his mutant powers into the open, they can then enslave him as a super-villain to do their nefarious bidding. The protracted montage of how Deadpool is tortured makes for difficult viewing as he is variously electrocuted, beaten, and maimed. Snarky Deadpool can't help himself as he mocks those torturing him, thinking he'll just eventually die. So their tortures become more diabolical. In one scene, the primary villain straps Deadpool into a hyperbaric chamber that constantly takes our anti-hero to the edge of asphyxiation before giving him oxygen — all with the quip that he enjoy his weekend. Over and beyond watching such physical torture, what's difficult for the audience, for me at least, is the film's willingness to represent those who delight in their seeming willingness to torture another human being. What's frightening about *Deadpool* is precisely this gratuitous display of not just the ability of some people to inflict harm on others but their *desire* to do so. Curiously enough, this last particular torture (in the hyperbaric chamber) works, and Deadpool's mutant regenerative abilities manifest— and, in the process, his entire body is scarred, his face disfigured, his flesh bearing the hideous sign of his superpower. He has become nearly invincible, but he will now forever look monstrous.

Deadpool becomes a perverse story about how extreme pain, cruel suffering, and extraordinary violation can become the source of one's ultimate power. Even more perversely, such suffering and violation becomes a lifetime of abuse accepted, a body penetrated, with the promise that it will survive, will regenerate, will persist. One wonders if the benefit of such persistence is too costly. But, in an increasing age of uncertainty for many people, perhaps this is the best story that can be offered. You won't be a morally uncompromised superhero and save the planet, but you *might* be able to learn to withstand the constant assaults on your mind and body, however monstrous such survival might make you. You can persist, even learn to make a life, but first you have to accept the torture on offer. And it won't stop, but at least you'll be alive. Of course, *Deadpool* is ultimately a (kinda sorta) superhero movie, and if he doesn't quite save the planet, he at least gets to defeat some of the bad guys. But his story is really about how the down-and-out have few options, even in the seemingly wealthiest and most democratic nation on the planet, but to accept the torture at hand — the shit jobs, the limited access to resources, the bad food, the daily grind, the promise of more of the same. *Deadpool* has the potential to speak to many folks, offering them snark as a coping mechanism, as a defense, as their bodies and minds suffer. (Perhaps this is why my trainer wouldn't watch it; perhaps it struck too close to home.)

I'm fortunate, so very fucking fortunate, that my work isn't a daily grind, that the suffering I encounter from the necessity of making a living is minor in comparison to that of so many, many others. But Deadpool's permeable body feels familiar. No, I've not been tortured. Or perhaps I have been, if not somatically then psychically. Going to school, day-in-day-out, treated to a ceaseless round of fag, faggot, queer, cocksucker, etc., etc. — that's a long-term kind of torture. Sustained bullying. And then, periodically, the more intense threats, the promise that, if possible, more direct harm could be visited upon my person. All of that builds up. So yes, a kind of prolonged torture.

I wonder, were these bullies trying to find my superpower? The question sounds absurd to me as soon as I write it. But in a way, the comparison isn't all that absurd. Learning to nourish and then even cherish my queerness, the thing that was tormented and tortured, has been, as we say, empowering. It has become a source of strength, and even pleasure. Bullies might have tried to penetrate, even violate the softest, most vulnerable part of me — the way in which I was drawn to others, my disposition toward intimacy with and erotic attachment to other boys. *That* part of me was tortured by the endless name-calling, threats, demeaning comments. But it continued to grow. And in time, it has become a way for me to regenerate myself.

I remember being in my mid-twenties, recently divorced, committing myself to a more openly queer life. I was barely "out of the closet," still unsure of myself, perhaps even wondering if I'd made the right decision. The trauma of torture clung to my psyche, manifesting in how I carried myself, a bit hunched over for a tall guy. But I was taking those first steps. I'm walking down a flight of stairs on my campus, the place I was first offered a teaching gig. I pass by a cute guy, probably not much younger than I am, and I turn momentarily as he passes, eyeing his tight ass in his tight jeans. And I think to myself, *this is good.* I love being able to see a great ass. It's a pleasure, even a fucking privilege, to catch a glimpse, however passing, of a guy in tight jeans, with a generous behind, glutei flexing as he walks up the stairs. This is good. This *is* good.

I think this was the first time my primary reaction to noting something on another man — a body part, a smile, a gesture, a way of being in the world — wasn't first and foremost, immediately, one of self-loathing, or shame, or even fear, particularly the fear that the man in question would notice me noticing and then want to beat the shit out of me, or at the very least dismiss me with a name, a label, a designation of contempt: *fucking faggot.*

In a way, my understanding of my queerness, of my own desires, had begun to mutate. Curiously, Deadpool is a mutant. In the Marvel universe, mutants are those famously meant for extermination, an aberration in the development and evolution of humanity. Indeed, one obvious metaphorical comparison the Marvel story offers is that between mutants and queers, both of whom eventually "manifest" their "powers" and are shunned, punished, and even at times rounded up for imprisonment, correction, and slaughter. The mutant metaphor is mobile, which is part of its power; who doesn't have something to hide, something inside that, if others only knew, would mark one as outcast, unclean, deserving of punishment. And how could I as a kid not respond to such a metaphor, feeling myself outcast, unclean, deserving of punishment?

The Marvel narratives work over the mutant metaphor, spinning out various permutations and possibilities that map onto "difference" writ large. Some mutants, notably those led by the powerful Dr. Xavier, rescue mutants in an attempt to save them, not just from those hostile to them, but in many cases from themselves. Dr. Xavier is often successful, but not always. For some, he's able to create a home, a school for the gifted, a place where their abilities can be nurtured, where they can be taught how to control and direct their powers for the good. Other mutants, led by Magneto, have decided that their powers can help them eradicate the humans who have bullied, hunted, punished, and killed them. This is the somewhat binary world that Marvel offers for dealing with "difference," for being an outsider: you're either an assimilationist or a terrorist; you're Dr. Martin Luther King or Malcolm X. Sexually, you're the Human Rights Campaign or the Lesbian Furies.

Some mutants, however, such as Wolverine, even Deadpool, remain more conflicted. Wolverine *often* choses to do good, but his is sometimes a compromised good, with fallout, damage, not-quite-intended destruction left in his wake. Deadpool too remains something of an outsider. The movies make it clear that at least some of Dr. Xavier's mutants would like Deadpool to join their ranks. But he hasn't yet. He won't assimilate. The damage is too deep, perhaps. The scars can't be forgotten or made beautiful — the scars that riddle his body, the outward signs of his torture that will never go away. Perhaps this is why I'm attracted to Deadpool as a character. I'm not a particularly good gay: I don't go to the right clubs or buy the right clothes or listen to the right music; and I don't contribute to Human Rights Campaign and I think that gays in the military and gay marriage are not unimportant but certainly not the *most* important rights we could be fighting for, especially when economic inequality and bullying for sexual and gender nonconformity are still killing people — sometimes slowly, sometimes all too quickly. I don't value assimilation, but I'm also not a terrorist. I'm political, and queerly so, but I enjoy my straight friends; hell, most of my friends are straight, and while I want them to acknowledge their privilege, I don't wish them dead, or in concentration camps.

The fact is I'm just damaged. Scarred. Some will say that I nurture the scars. They wouldn't be wrong. This is the second book that I'm writing about my damage. I don't think I'll ever not write about it. Perhaps I've just come to recognize those scars, that damage, as a kind of strength. Not a superpower, but yes, a way to nurture a particular kind of growth, or at least a particular kind of vision of the world. Others don't need to join my cause. I don't think I even have a cause. But I'm here, part of the world, so I'm also part of you. And I make witness to what has been done to me, what has been taken from me, what suffering I have borne, what monstrous births come out of my deep nourishing of that history of suffering.

You can pet those monsters if you want. You're petting them now, having read this far. I hope they scare you. They are testimony to the permeability of all of our bodies, to the ways in which we can all be violated, the ways in which we are, to some extent, all constantly violated by the culture around us. Our bodies and minds are all permeable to the machinations of capital, the flows of greed, the desires for *more* — more control, more access, more power, more wealth, more influence, more and more. Some of us have learned to fetishize our permeability. Every week I check out a Tumblr account, Marvel Heroes in Peril, a site devoted to cartoon images of various superheroes in states of bondage, distress, and pain. Someone else out there, and many others too considering the number of responses to the site, are checking out the torture of our superheroes. Their bodies, as strong as they are, as mutant and mutated, are subject still to further mutilation. They are in pain. They are all of us in pain, even our heroes, pained and suffering. We imagine even the strongest of us, pained and suffering. Why would I, so not very strong, why would I not watch, marvel, take solace, even delight?

We learn to love our pain.

***

Negotiating out consensual power exchange is a tricky thing. I know deeply after much reflection that my interest in kink stems from early violation, from a need to return to the point where someone is exercising control over me and yet, in the context of "play," I have agreed to the control and thus maintain some control over it myself. It's a complicated puzzle here, a maze in which I'm faking myself out, reliving again and again the not undelicious feeling of being out of control, but this time doing it safely. I put it to myself this way sometimes: I'm being punished but I'm determining the contours, limits, and boundaries of that punishment. Someone is going to hurt me, but I'm going to know how much, and I can say *stop*.

Unless I can't.

My particular kink became for a while in my youth pushing this boundary — *where do I stop? Where should I stop? I'm* not insane. I don't want to be harmed. But if I'm truly being punished, if I'm to relive what it's like to experience someone's control over me, then the scripting of the event can't be entirely pre-determined, completely in my control. It's a razor-blade difference here, cutting too many ways. But for a while in my twenties I kept approaching that blade, fingering it, wondering how deeply I could split the difference here.

Once I contracted with an older man for a spanking session. I say "contract" because it definitely felt like a contract, a literal negotiating-out ahead of time of what we're interested in, what he wants to do, what I'm willing to withstand and tolerate, what I would actually *like* him to do, what he's comfortable administering. We exchanged lots and lots of emails to set something like this up. Part of the pleasure of the impending scene emerged just in those exchanges, the ramping up of talk as we each imagined the scenario, the scene, the drama we were writing.

Who this particular man is isn't totally relevant here. Surely in some version of this narrative it is. But he was just like any number of other men that I would meet up with at times to play out these scenes. Inevitably he was older though I'm going to resist identifying him as paternal or fatherly. He likely *was* a father but my conversations with these men rarely advanced to the point of exchanging such intimate details. I do remember this particular man, though, telling me that his wife would kill him if she ever found out that he met up with boys to spank them. I don't doubt it. I can only imagine what psychic drama he was playing out in his own mind as he emailed me furtively to talk about my impending punishment. Our transferential monsters drive us at times to surprising destinations.

We met after work hours at the industrial site that he seemed to manage. Again, I had few details and I wasn't inquiring. He wasn't inquiring too much about me either. The town was small and the likelihood of running into each other "in public" wasn't out of the question. The "scene," though, was interesting, one I'd never played in before; usually such games are confined to bedrooms, apartments, interior locales. It would be interesting to be punished in a warehouse.

And he made good advantage of the area. After a little bit of warm-up spanking over my khaki shorts, he led me into the warehouse proper, over to a wooden scaffold, where he told me to take off my shorts and then handcuffed me, in white briefs and a t-shirt, to the scaffold. My hands were tied to a low beam so I had to squat down. He walked around admiring my predicament, and then told me to lift up my rear, which he paddled slowly, deliberately. I was totally turned on. I'm aroused just remembering this scene from so long ago. Cuffed, humiliated in jump my underpants, I had to raise my bottom up to be spanked, as though lifting my butt was a way of asking for it to be punished.

Eventually he uncuffed me and we continued our play in various positions. He even at one point had me walk around the warehouse, naked, picking up cigarette butts. Being forced to do such a disgusting task doesn't strike me as quite as erotic in retrospect as it might have during the scene itself. The level of erotic intensity comes and goes in such play, wave-like. I'm always struck by the stray bits and pieces that surface later, stimulating me, twitching my cock, becoming fodder for masturbation. I don't think I've ever jerked off to the cigarette butts, though. Lifting my ass up for a paddling? Yes. And then the next bit — more complicated, but yes.

We'd been playing for about an hour, my ass getting tired of the beatings. He could probably tell I was winding down. He wanted me to suck him off, but I'd already said in our negotiations that I didn't want any overt sexual contact. I wasn't going to give him a blow job and didn't expect one in turn. In my mind, our play was purely about power exchange, about whipping my ass. He could jerk off or fuck his wife and think about blistering my butt later if he wanted.

He led me back to the wooden scaffolding and cuffed my hands with me standing upright now, my legs spread and tied to the bottom beam. A little more spanking, he said. Almost caressing now, and I definitely thought we were winding down.

He then put his hand on my shoulder and said, "Ok, ten final licks with the strap. And it's going to be hard. It's going to hurt."

I started to panic. I was already red, bruised. I'd had enough. I didn't want any more. His caressing my ass had led me to believe that we were just about done. But I was trapped, cuffed to the scaffold and there was nothing I could do. The thought hit me: *I'm going to be punished for real now.* I started to beg, "No, sir, please, no more. I can't take any more."

He stood back and slashed his belt, hard, across my ass. I shouted out. Again, and again, each forceful stroke delivered with deliberation, my shouts of pain and panic all but ripped from me. He was inflicting pain. He knew it. He enjoyed it. It hurt so much. I continued shouting out, nearly screaming, begging for him to stop.

Then it was over. He put his hand back on my shoulder. "Boy, your ass is *so* red." He uncuffed me and I stepped back, putting my hands on my naked thighs to catch my breath, bent over, still submissive.

I'd been pushed, as kinksters say, beyond my limits. In that moment, I was totally ready to go, even a little bit scared of this older, gray-haired man, likely someone's father. No, I told him, I still wasn't going to blow him, so I started to pack up my paddles and cuffs and got dressed. We were cordial, but I knew that I wouldn't play with him again.

For decades, I've thought about this scene. It's gotten me off many nights. It still can.

I wouldn't do it again.

**

Yesterday I got my second tattoo. Mack and I trained up to Union Station from our home in Orange County, then took the Metro subway out to Studio City, to the same tattoo parlor where I had my first tattoo done almost three years ago. We had a late breakfast, waiting for the parlor to open, then walked over and asked for the tattoo. The shop is decked out in various pirate gear, skulls and crossbones everywhere, glass cases resplendent with gold jewelry, and a full-size human torture cage tucked in one corner. Tattoo parlors always seem to me to cut the difference between (on one hand) barber shop, with vinyl reclining chairs everywhere and stands full of equipment within easy reach, and (on the other hand) bondage shop, with vinyl reclining chairs everywhere and stands full of equipment within easy reach. The staggered drilling of the inking machines also eerily recalls dental offices, imparting something of a sense of dread but also promising that you are really, ultimately, here to take care of yourself. You're doing something good for your body, even if it's going to hurt a bit.

Am I doing something good for my body?

I never, as in never ever, wanted a tattoo and my interest in body modification was perhaps, maybe, limited to thoughts about getting a pierced ear. *Maybe.* I was intellectually intrigued by body mod as a form of sadomasochistic practice, but piercing, puncturing, scarring, and inking all seemed a bit too permanent. These are activities *beyond* play. They are commitments. I could enjoy some play, but I wanted out at some point. I wanted to be able to tell the man strapping my ass, "Ok, enough, thank you. Banana. Banana!"

But about three years ago, staying in my mother's house one Christmas, spending a little bit of time with her and other family, I had a vision. I'm not kidding. I characterized it as a download into my brain, something along the order of what I imagine the science fiction writer Philip K. Dick experienced when he claimed that a beam of pink light shot the secret knowledge of history into his brain, telling him that we are all still living in the depths of the Roman Empire but just don't know it. Ok, perhaps my download wasn't that comprehensive. But I very much felt that I was called to get a tattoo — and that that tattoo would be of a gecko, in solid black ink, on my upper left arm, and that I would get that tattoo the coming summer, before my forty-ninth birthday.

A byproduct of paranoia, of feeling that the next round of abuse or violation is just around the corner, often comes with the corollary sense that, when you receive a clear vision of something you should do, then you should do it. If the world promises to hurt you, as it had so often promised me in the past, then when it actually offers you a chance to do something a little bit unusual or different, then perhaps you should partake of the opportunity, given that, otherwise, you are pretty much only (or at least usually) promised pain.

The rub of course is that getting a tattoo is painful. Actually, that's not the rub. That may be the *point*. I received a clear call, a direct download, that offered me the chance to experience a very particular kind of pain, in a very particular kind of way and at a predesignated time — all of which I could control. So of course, I had to do it. It's as though my brain had been cogitating over how it could offer me the possibility of getting a tattoo in such a way that I would experience the pain of the procedure but would also understand it as safe and even desirable. The fact that I would get it right before my birthday, the commencement of my ultimate year in my forties, and that it would be a gecko — these were just perfect. My mind knew exactly how to tempt me into doing this thing, this somewhat permanent thing that I would do to my body, this way to mark me, this way to mark myself, to violate my own skin, but under my control, to my specifications, to my own desires.

The gecko has long been my spirit animal, and I'm aware that I say that with some trepidation. I am not of Indigenous lineage, but I fell in love with the gecko design when I lived in Colorado — the curved gecko, rounding in on its own tail, symbol both of the circular and repeating nature of our existence, but also of survival, even at a cost, the little lizard who can survive in the harshest of desert climates and who, when preyed upon, is wiling to leave behind an appendage, a tail, so that its predator can have a snack while the gecko flees to safety. That was me. That was me, even as I wasn't sure at the time, in my twenties, living in Colorado, having fled Louisiana, having fled into a marriage with a woman, even as I wasn't sure what *of myself* I had actually left behind. I thought I had survived a hostile place — as I had — and that what I'd left behind was pain, intolerance, abuse, victimization. I didn't know yet the extent to which I carried these things with me.

I didn't know yet what I still carried with me.

Once, on another visit to my mother, before I had the tattoo, before I had received the vision to get the tattoo but long still into my identification with the gecko, I'm in the back room, packing my bag, and I hear my mother start to screen and shout, yipping loudly with alarm. I rush out, "What's wrong? What's wrong?!"

"Oh! There's a gecko, look! There's a gecko! Get it out! Get it out! Kill it!"

I immediately started laughing. There was no way she could've known how much I identified with that little gecko, or even really what a spirit animal is. That's not a part of any culture to which she'd been substantially exposed. So I laughed and laughed all the while I got a broom and swept the little lizard off the wall, gently moving it toward the door, a little lizard, reddish, banded, likely frightened and then leaving its tail behind as it scampered out the door. I swept the tail out after it, my laughter turning to chuckles turning to a knowing nod as my mother's hysterics settled down. She wouldn't know how much I felt I was sweeping myself right out that door, or how that tail, that small precious bit left behind, spoke to me.

What have you left behind? What have you had to abandon to save yourself?

So, a gecko, a survivor. Something my mother hated to have in her house. In the moment, I couldn't resist the weird parallels, even as I know my mother loves me. I *know* my mother loves me. I love her. And now I love the gecko tattoo, in solid black, on my upper left arm. I couldn't *not* get it. Few things have seemed to be just so right. And it didn't hurt much. Some, yes, for sure, especially when Dan, the tattoo artist, a young blond kid, started shading it in after having inked the outline. I'd taken a Klonopin and applied the numbing gel a couple of hours before. All good. Enough pain for my body to know that something was happening, something a bit foreign being injected beneath my skin, my skin over the next week wanting to push out the ink, leaving a stark black imprint of the gecko on my white towels when I washed. But the skin ultimately accepted the ink, keeping enough of the gecko shape so that it's unmistakable, a marking, a bit of body art, a modification to my skin, suggestive I felt of the interior modifications I've gone through to get this far, just on the edge of forty-nine, a survivor. I purposefully marked myself, Cain, an outcast, but still here. I purposefully violated my body, an echo of past violations, but this time under my control, at my direction, a thing I've done to myself, a thing of violation but also of beauty. A thing now to attract attention. Sometimes people want to touch it. I sometimes let them.

But now, yesterday, Mack and I go up for another tattoo. I'd had another vision, this time a bit less insistent, a bit less particular, more a compelling idea, something I would definitely do if given the chance. *What, though, is given? When one has an idea, one either gives oneself the chance or one doesn't.* I took this reasoning as an opportunity to be even more deliberate about this tattoo. If my mind had sent me the earlier vision as a provocation to act, even a demand that I do this thing however under my control doing it would ultimately be, it now offered me the chance to decide all the more self consciously. So I took that opportunity. I would have the words "Je est un autre" inked on my inner forearm.

Je est un autre.

I is an other. These are the words with which the young, the terribly young nineteenth-century French poet Arthur Rimbaud announces to a few people, including a former teacher, that he fully intends to break all the rules of poetry in the creation of a new language, a language he believed would transform the world, turning it inside out, but only after turning himself inside out. He advocated for the "rational disarranging of the senses" as a means for questioning—radically, deeply, permanently—all of the received wisdom of the world, a path to clear out space in the soul, in the mind, in the body for a new way of being, a being we could only glimpse at now but that, in time and with a new language, we would realize through our very flesh. It would be a way of being of fullness, richness, exuberant totality, realizing the scents of colors, the colors of vowels, the soulful touch of everything sensuous and material. In the process, Rimbaud would escape the stifling confines of his rural bourgeois family and schooling. He'd flee to Paris and cavort with other poets. He'd remake himself into the "other" that he could only imagine as a boy. He'd break the rules—even the rules of grammar—to become this other person.[4]

I is an other.

Rimbaud made it to Paris, where his brilliance shocked those around him. He was uncouth, foul, difficult, but captivating, even mesmerizing. The married-with-child poet Paul Verlaine fell under his spell, the two embarking on a strange erotic odyssey, running away to try to make a life together in England before winding up back in France, then Brussels, where Verlaine shot Rimbaud when the younger man started to leave him, dissatisfied with the relationship. Perhaps too much disarrangement, or an overly clingy Verlaine. Rimbaud survived the gunshot, just a flesh wound, and went on to write both the poems included in *Illuminations,* the stunning prose poems of transcendent vision that seemed to be the verse articulations of a rational disarrangement of the senses, but also *A Season in Hell,* in which Rimbaud captures in some of the finest poetic language of the nineteenth century the paradoxical inability of language to usher in the new world, a new way of being. *Season* tracks his descent, his dissolution, the botched relationship with Verlaine, the failure of poetry, in exquisite verse, a language of beautiful

---

4   There are many accounts of Arthur Rimbaud's life and works. I'd recommend, for starters, Edmund White's lovely and short *Rimbaud: The Double Life of a Rebel,* published in 2008.

failure. And then Rimbaud stopped writing, at twenty-one years of age, having produced masterpieces. He would eventually become a gun runner in what is modern-day Ethiopia, ultimately losing his leg to what was likely bone cancer and dying at 37, likely never having written anything literary again.

Je est un autre.

I wrote a third of my dissertation on Rimbaud, one of three poets I was obsessed with as a young man. I loved his story, not just his verse. I loved — I still love — the yearning, the striving, the great attempt to remake himself, the "descent" into a homosexual relationship, even drug abuse and violence. I loved Rimbaud because, in my early twenties, I believed he had done all of the things that I would never do, that I might have wanted to do, but that I wouldn't. And, of course, he was also a cautionary tale. Look what had happened to him. You can't remake the world with your words. You can try, but you can't. At most, you'll leave behind the tortured tale of your attempt. You could write about your season in hell, but don't forget: *it was still in hell.* So I loved this story, his story, this cautionary tale, this warning, this bad boy who couldn't escape punishment, no matter how far away he ran, even to Africa. But really, also really, I thrilled to the attempt, to the boldness, the brazen attempt to be other than what he was.

I is an other.

What was less clear to me at the time was that Rimbaud, having arrived in Paris as a kid, still a teenager, was likely homeless and begging, likely even raped by a group of soldiers, an experience that one of Rimbaud's early biographer, Enid Starkie, says might have awakened him to his sexuality. But was he actually raped? Later biographers are less sure. Perhaps Starkie, writing in 1936, couldn't understand anal penetration as something that a young man, a much younger man, would willingly undergo. So this early experience, this penetration of the young boy — is it a violation, or an invitation? Later, Rimbaud and Verlaine would write a poem "To the Asshole," which my friend George Lang has translated:

Dark, squinched up like the bud of a violet,
it breathes humbly, tucked among tuffs of moss
which follow the slope still slick with love's gloss
from pale ass cheek to the rim of its eyelet.

Filaments like tears of cream cry out askant
against gusts of foul wind driving them astray
through fields strewn with clots of reddish clay
till they peter out down the enticing slant.

My dream is to butt to its suction cup.
My soul, for actual coitus hard up,
seeks out this gutter, this nest of tears.

Swooning olive gland, flute for which to pine,
tube from which slides celestial praline,
a feminine Canaan within a mat of hairs.[5]

Raped or not raped. Violated or not. Definitely shot at, definitely
having undergone a strange if purportedly rational derange-
ment, a studied attempt to undo the bourgeois boy he had been.
Definitely someone who enjoyed his asshole, at least in some
cases, and perhaps in all of them. For a time. Before giving all of
it up and pursuing dreams of money, adventure, different kinds
of danger.

I am not Rimbaud. I am *so* not Rimbaud. But the boy who
wrote about him in his dissertation, the cautionary tale, the
beautiful but dangerous attempt to transform the world through
language, through desire, through the body, even through deg-
radation — that boy wouldn't go as far as Rimbaud, but he would
go far enough. He would become other. He would slowly figure
out how to pursue the desires burbling up in his soul, running

---

5   George Lang's translation is used with permission. George translates
several poems (by Rimbaud and others) and posts them to his site: https://
alteritas.net. I am in his debt for many conversations about Rimbaud, and
wine.

under his skin, sifting his dreams into shame and possibility. *I is an other.* He wouldn't know what that other would ultimately look like, what that other is still becoming, how that other is always displaced into dream, shame, but also possibility and pursuit. He would give some space to that other, those others, those possibilities. He would remember the cautionary tale. He would remember the voices, the threats, the doctrine, the words spoken with Christian love that try to keep the other, the others, at a distance, that want to banish those others to the places where there is only weeping and gnashing of teeth. Those voices would also be his others. *I is an other.* I, after all, is also the voices given, the voices implanted, the voices all but inked on the skin, running along the skin that also wants to touch, to taste, to feel the things desired, the things denied, the things forbidden. I is always all of these voices.

So he is still becoming other, trying to become other to the vision given him, given him, so he gives to himself the other, in small ways, admittedly such small ways, but in ways he thinks he can survive.

I sit in the chair in this tattoo parlor in Studio City, and the same boy who gave me my gecko nearly three years ago is, surprise surprise, about to give me my new tattoo on my exposed and now shaved forearm. The same boy, Dan, blond, a little bit older than last time but not much. This feels like the universe's way of saying *you will do this, you will do this thing.* I had not asked for him. I didn't remember his name. I had not anticipated that he would even still be working here. But here he is. The same boy, assigned to me. When you are paranoid, you also take such coincidences as sign, as affirmation, as the universe —this time—actually cooperating with you, not just trying to hurt you. Dan will hurt me. I will forego the Klonopin and the cocktail and the numbing gel. I will feel for this hour the words scratched into my skin. It will hurt. I have asked to be hurt. Purposefully, with meaning this time, with the words I have chosen. With the violation I give myself.

***

I'm sitting with Elizabeth Loftus, a colleague on my campus, a famous psychologist, someone who studies memory, someone who has given testimony in numerous court cases about the flexibility, malleability, and impermanence of memory. We forget. We more than forget; we fabricate unknowingly.[6] Here's our conversation, transcribed:

JA: This project is, in part, about my uncle. I believed for a long time that I was sexually molested by him when I was a child.

EL: You're kidding.

JA: No.

EL: When did you start believing that?

JA: Um… My early twenties… and that persisted for… for some time.

EL: Were you in therapy?

JA: I was in therapy for a little while.

EL: Mmmm.

JA: I very much understood at the time that, maybe, perhaps as a reason that me, myself, in my teens and early twenties was experiencing strong attractions to men. So, believing that he had sexually molested me…

EL: Oh, that, that was…

JA: …was a way to understand my own homosexuality in a particularly homophobic culture and time. I don't know if he did or

---

6 For more on Dr. Elizabeth Loftus, see her Wikipedia entry: https://en.wikipedia.org/wiki/Elizabeth_Loftus.

not. There was a moment when I was a child when I believe this may have taken place... uh... my parents sort of corroborated that they felt something strange had happened but that they weren't sure what it was. So, I have no clear memory of the abuse having taken place but I have a strong sense that this happened, and it came about, the sense came about in my early twenties, right when I was about to be married to a young woman, and as I was grappling with my own feelings of homosexuality...

EL: Oh, wow, so you were engaged actually in...

JA: I was engaged; yes, yes...

EL: And feeling like something wasn't right...

JA: And feeling like something wasn't right... and knew that I had attractions to men but was thinking this is why; my path toward normalcy had somehow been derailed, but I als--

EL: Wait — can I —

JA: Yeah. Absolutely. Ask any question you want.

EL: I'm just, because I know a lot about this sort of history...

JA: Yeah.

EL: I'm just trying to get to what year this would have been and how old you would have been, because this explosion of the idea that abuse was the source of whatever your problems and issues were exploded in the early '90s, and that seems a little early for you...

JA: No; this would have been '91, '92, '93...

EL: So, that's... OK, that's interesting...

JA: Yeah.

EL: OK…

JA: Um… it is, interesting.

EL: Yeah…

JA: What was going on then? In '91, '92… what was happening in the early '90s?

EL: That was really the beginning of what we now call the "memory wars," where…

JA: Mmm hmmm.

EL: …people were coming up with these new memories or beliefs or whatever-you-want-to-call-them that they were molested; they now wanted to take action against their abusers — but they were prevented from doing so by the statute of limitations.

JA: Ahh, uh huh.

EL: So, starting with… I don't know where you were living then…

JA: In Louisiana.

EL: Oh, OK. Well, at the time some states were starting to roll back the statutes of limitations, and, if you claimed you repressed your memory and now it was back, that started the clock, and you could sue your alleged abuser. That was '89. California did it in '91, and then, you know, within a few years, twelve states. I don't remember where Louisiana fits, but that was when we started to see this explosion of cases of people with their newfound memories of abuse and it was all in the culture, these buried recalcitrant trauma memories were the cause of all your issues... perfect timing... but go on...

JA: It's fascinating, because I did not remember that, uh, bit of history. I definitely think that as a victim of very intense homophobic bullying, especially in middle school and high school, that I suffered sexual abuse, or a form of sexual abuse.

EL: Well, uh... You mean because of the bullying?

JA: Because of the bullying.

EL: Well, what...

JA: And, specifically, the homophobic nature of it.

EL: But why were you bullied? I mean why...

JA: Oh, well, it was very clear that I was not straight. Students... my classmates... definitely pegged me as queer.

EL: Was it mannerisms, or was it? What... what was it?

JA: Probably mannerisms. Um. General effeminacy.

EL: Hmm.

JA: Um, lack of interest in sports, and things of that nature. I was very shy, as well.

EL: Mmm.

JA: So, I, I understand that as a form of sexual abuse. Ah —

EL: Mmm.

JA: And you can imagine — growing up, grappling with feelings of attraction to men or other boys, ah, in a very homophobic environment…

EL: Mmm hmmm…

JA: And I think I may have just latched onto this, this narrative…

EL: Well, it was out there in the culture that…

JA: Yeah.

EL: That…

JA: Mmmm.

EL: Mostly for women who were looking for an explanation for their issues, their eating disorders, their depression, their anxiety, their whatever, not usually their lesbian…

JA: Mmmm. <inhales audibly> Do people repress memories?

EL: I teach a whole three-month graduate seminar called Memory and The Law.

JA: Yeah.

EL: There really isn't credible evidence for massive repression of severe trauma by some process. There's not thinking about things, even awful things, and being reminded, but…

JA: Ah.

EL: It's a major controversy. I have a fairly recent paper — "Are the Memory Wars Over?" And the answer is no. And it's a massive survey of different mental health and science professionals that shows the gap and the controversy, so psychoanalytically oriented, you know, hypnotherapists, they might tend to believe it's true…

JA: Yeah.

EL: But even the clinical researchers are skeptical.

JA: Yeah.

EL: But go on… back to your story…

JA: I think about this because part of me thinks, if this happened, I should have a memory of it. I have a memory of so many other things from my childhood, even from early childhood… so if this had happened, I would remember it. I wonder though if I have…

EL: Well, what memories do you have of your uncle?… Well, you wrote a book about this, [*Creep*] …

JA: Yeah… a lot of memories… of my, of my uncle. I even remember going to see *Fantasia* with him, which is supposedly the night that this incident would have taken place. I supposedly called or asked to call my mother and father, and wanted to go home, but they were out and about and didn't want to pick me up because I was staying with my uncle that night. Then later when I told them I might have been abused by him, they said, "Oh, we should have gone to pick you up that night."

EL: Oh.

JA: So, I don't have a sense —

EL: Have you ever looked up to see when *Fantasia* was released?

JA: Ah, well this would have been a re-release, ah…

EL: Oh, a re-release.

JA: At some point in the early '70s, so I would have been 5... 6... 7...

EL: You were born in?

JA: '67.

EL: OK.

JA: So, I actually remember going to see *Fantasia*. I have memories of going to see that with him. I don't have memories of calling my parents, though. And, I don't have memories of the abuse, so whether or not it happened I think will always, in some ways, be a question mark. But I'm compelled by this sense that the narrative of the abuse became powerful for me in the early '90s, right when I'm about to be married...

EL: Mmmm....

JA: And, as you say, right when there's a larger cultural narrative...

EL: Mmm hmm.

JA: ...about the power of repressed memories.

EL: So... I'm sort of asking this, like, as your friend, out of curiosity... now that you know, as the big grown-up Jonathan...

JA: Mm hmm.

EL: ...that people are gay and they're not sexually abused, you know... that's not a typical route [to becoming gay]... do you... what is your motivation for wanting to figure this out? You don't need... You're not thinking about... You're happy with the way you are now. You like your life, and...

JA: Yeah.

EL: And so... what is the purpose of this?

JA: <inhales and exhales> I think the purpose of this, of telling this particular story, of probing this story, would be to document how desperate I was not to be gay.

EL: Mmm.

JA: And that I would go to the extent to create this narrative about an uncle whom I otherwise loved dearly.

EL: Mmm.

JA: And that that is what living in a homophobic time and place can do to one. It can, it can... potentially twist how one feels about a relative, or about a loved person.

EL: So... I mean I think this is all quite reasonable and likely. Your motive was to explain this and all these cases I've been involved in since the early '90s... they have another reason for wanting to believe that Daddy did horrible things to them.

JA: What was it?

EL: An explanation for their problems.

JA: Yeah.

EL: You know... possible explanations for their eating disorder, anxiety, depression... promiscuity... whatever, you know... it doesn't matter. Either you're a bad person... well, one of my clinician friends said it's either A, B, or C. C, you're crazy; nobody wants that. B, you're a bad person; no one wants that. A, you're abused. And it's a great explanation. I mean, this is my answer when people ask, "Why would anyone want to believe that Daddy did something so horrible, if it's not true?" and I say, "Well, you know, there's a cost to it, because it broke up the family. You didn't do that but these families break up with these accusations, so there must be a benefit; let's figure out the benefit."

JA: Well, certainly, I knew my parents desperately did not want me to be gay.

EL: Mm hmm.

JA: So being able to blame my uncle, who was dead by that point, he was a sort of convenient blame…

EL: Was he your mother's brother?

JA: Yeah, my mother's brother. He was an easy… and openly gay himself…

EL: Mmm hmmm.

JA: …he was an easy way for me to put blame on somebody for things that I felt…

EL: Yeah.

JA: …that I didn't have to then own. Because if I'd owned that, claimed that, as my own desires, then that would've really been devastating to both of my parents.

EL: Mmm hmm. Um… *<many package-opening sounds, then sounds of nuts twinkling into the bowl>* You know, I mean, I've spent most of my last god-knows-how-long defending accused people. I'd be working on behalf of the uncle after you sued him or got him prosecuted, you know? I, I…

<pause>

Now, I mean, you know, the… *<pause>*

I don't know. I mean, I, I… you don't need this… I mean, I don't… I'm not even sure what to say. So, I mean, I get involved in the court cases where it is so heavily disputed and the person is denying it, and…

JA: Yeah.

EL: And it sounds like if he were alive he'd deny it.

JA: Uh…

EL: And maybe it would even, if he were alive, lead to a break-up with his sister…

JA: Mmm.

EL: If you insisted…

JA: Yeah.

EL: That everybody believe you…

JA: Yeah.

EL: …and he insisted everyone believed the denial, and…

JA: Yeah. Maybe one of the reasons I'm working on this material is, in part, to vindicate him.

EL: Oh. For. Mmm. Did anyone ever, in all these years, accuse him of anything?

JA: No.

EL: Hmm. *<sounds of nuts cracking>*

JA: But vindicate him in terms of my own thinking…

EL: Oh, OK, but not in terms of the family history, or…

JA: Right.

EL: Well, then, one thing I could ask you is, why are you talking to me, because I, you could've anticipated that, I'm going to be somebody who's going to be skeptical.

JA: I think that's exactly why I'm talking to you. <laughs>

EL: *<laughs>*

JA: *<hearty laugh>*

EL: *<laugh>*

JA: I think that's precisely why I'm talking to you.

***

Just recently, I unfriended someone on Facebook — I know, I know, such a petty thing to do, and I was a little bit ashamed. But, then again, not. In the decade I've been on Facebook I've connected with a variety of kids from my old high school, although few of them people I might actually have counted as my friends while in high school. Still, a number of young men have become FB "friends," yet another variety of relationality spawned by our connected world. Most of these folks I didn't really know well in high school, some of them pretty tangentially, and even a couple I can't recall at all, though I accept the friendships and the obligatory Messenger chats that are quick catch-ups — *you good? yeah, I'm good. I'm good too!*

But one young man — funny, I call him a young man, when he is my age, pretty much exactly my age — someone I do recall, though we were never friends, I unfriended. He had posted a picture of an attractive young blonde woman force-feeding another attractive young woman a bottle, with the caption reading something along the lines of "The LGBT community stuffing their sexuality down our throats." It was a disgusting meme. I was repulsed — perhaps especially by how the image perversely deployed its infantilist eroticism to malign queer people. Even more to the point of my disgust, the sentiment here just got everything wrong. Yes, some queers are flamboyant, and our demands for various equal rights and, well, freedom from living in fear, have likely struck some as "outrageous" — but really, *what the fuck* — I've lived my entire life, especially as a child growing up in a christian culture and attending christian schools, having not just heterosexuality thrust down my throat, but also being force-fed a steady diet of self-hatred. The irony intensifies as I think about all the claims that queers recruit and that young people better watch out. Again, *are you fucking kidding me?* Christians recruit. Let's be clear. *Christians recruit.* Their god tells them to go make other christians. So claims of queer recruitment and how LGBT folks force their sexuality down the throats of others are quite simply *projection*. Christians accuse us of what they have done for so long, so very long, immiserating the lives of countless millions of people over time.

Do you wonder why I have thought that christianity, much like all religion that has evangelical fervor and fundamentalist dimensions, should be banned from civil society? Christians indoctrinate children. I refer to their churches and their schools as indoctrination camps. They twist as many souls as they claim to save — and I say that knowing, knowing in my heart, that they have indeed helped some people, that they have at times fed the poor, healed the sick, offered comfort to the weary and despairing — *but at what cost? At what fucking cost to the rest of us?* As a friend once put it to me, "We cannot celebrate a culture and a people who comfort with one hand while concussing with the other."

So I unfriended this person because I didn't want this bullshit appearing in my feed. In my fifty years on this planet, I've heard enough of this, and I have fought to get to the place where I can say *no, I just don't have to listen to this shit,* much less be exposed to it when I'm otherwise just going about my business.

But I took another step. I am friends on FB with one of the administrators of the old high school I suffered through, someone I knew when I was attending this high school so long ago. So I contacted him and told him this story, the story of the unfriending, and why I had done it, and how I hoped that times were changing enough so that young men, perhaps some young men who might be like me, would not have to endure the abuse I had. I sent two messages through Messenger. Here is the first one.

Mr. XXX — my FB feed says that you're in retreat with other XXX faculty. I wish you all the best. I write, out of the blue, because I recently took the very rare step of unfriending someone on FB a couple of days ago. A high school classmate posted a picture complaining about members of the LGBT community jamming sexuality down the throats of everyone else. You'll have to excuse my vitriol if I respond by saying that I've never seen anything the queer community has done that could compare to the way that homophobic heterosexuality was jammed down my throat nearly every day of my high school experience — by people calling me faggot, queer, homo. Unfortunately I know some faculty turned a blind eye. And I heard that one faculty member condoned this kind of treatment. And yet another actually told homophobic jokes in class. That I survived high school is the miracle for me. I know the religious orientation of XXX is intolerant of gays and lesbians, but I do hope your faculty will be mindful of the damage done to hearts and minds and souls through homophobia. If at any point you want to talk about this, I'm happy to do so. All best — j.

I received no response to this message, although I could tell through Messenger that it had been "seen." So I sent another one.

Mr. XXX —

I'm sorry if my message took you by surprise. I know you're about to start the new year, so my message was likely unwelcome. And to be fair, I respect the work that many faculty did when I attended XXX. AAA, BBB — they meant much to me, and I remember them fondly.

But the message from the classmate was triggering, for sure. I was bullied and abused by many classmates. They'd call my home and threaten me and my parents. And yes, unfortunately, some faculty — through turning away or through their own actions — were complicit. Not all, for sure. And I hold dearly the memories of those like AAA and BBB who tried to nurture me. But psychic violence perpetrated at that age, so consistently, is hard to forget.

In so many ways, I've had a great life. I've moved on, married, built a family and career. My husband and I have been together for over 20 years, and my fifteenth book comes out this fall. My mother lives with us now, and it's my delight to help take care of her in her final years.

But I remember. I feel the twitch of abuse under my skin, remembering the taunts, jeers, insults, threats. I have had to learn that it may never go away.

I am not inviting you to feel bad about this. I have no negative memories of you at all. But I saw your FB posting and wanted someone at XXX to know. I am a survivor. I am a gay survivor. I am a gay man, and, while I know it's asking for the impossible, I'd like someone at XXX to acknowledge that the homophobic abuse I endured should be endured by no one at a Christian school, regardless of the particular faith's beliefs on sexuality. As educators, we should protect our young people, and teach them not to savage one another. All of our students, straight or gay, deserve to know that they are loved and appreciated.

Times have changed, and are continuing to change. I remain hopeful.

So, what do I need from you? Nothing, though an acknowledgment would be appreciated. More than that, in my wildest dreams, Mr. XXX, you, as Director of Student Activities, could invite me to speak with your faculty. I'd gladly share my thoughts — cordially, collegially, respectfully. Or perhaps you invite me to dinner, maybe with AAA and others, just to chat. I'll actually be in Louisiana next month…

I wish you and your colleagues — and your students, all of them — all the best, Mr. XXX, as you begin this new academic year.

Again, I received no response to this query, though it had apparently been seen. I cannot deny disappointment in not having received at least a kind word in response. I know from another teacher with whom I'm still in some contact that the administrator shared my message, that there was some discussion about what might be possible. Good news, potentially, but nothing yet. I don't entertain much hope for movement.

But I feel the movement inside me. I feel my own openness. I feel myself moving toward possibility, connection. I am cautious, but not paranoid. At least not *always* paranoid. No, I have not repaired the damage done to me. I still grieve my childhood. But I don't let that grief—that grief given to me by a church, a school, a family, a culture—continue to abuse me. I offer myself — and these others, these who are guiding the lives of other people's children — I offer us the possibility of reparation. They haven't taken up my offer yet. But I offer.

It's not enough. I fear it will not be enough.

***

Dear Chancellor XXX and Provost XXX:

I write this morning after much thought this weekend about a truly unfortunate sign I saw while walking to work along Ring Road on Friday morning. The large poster, attached to this email, advertises an upcoming talk on campus by journalist Milo Yiannopoulos, sponsored by [two student groups]. I see many signs advertising events on campus, but what struck me was the large lettering asking, "Who are we to let such dangerous FAGGOTRY *go unpunished?" — with "*FAGGOTRY*" in red.*

I literally did a double take. I shut it out of my mind as soon as I read it, something in me wanting to close down for a moment. But I forced myself to stop, take a step back, and reread the sign. I had to do a little research to find out who Milo Yiannopoulos is, but I figure that's why we have smart phones. And then I used mine to take a picture of this poster so I could discuss it with colleagues. I walked to my first meeting of the day. I showed [a colleague] the picture who then immediately took action by alerting appropriate campus officials. I forwarded the picture to my colleagues in the Department of Gender and Sexuality Studies, who then also took action by alerting various units on campus.

Since then, my colleagues and I have been informed that the poster was approved for posting and that it falls within campus guidelines for posting. A few campus staff have attempted to talk to the young people who posted the sign about how potentially injurious the sign is to LGBT *folks on campus, but the students won't hear the concern. They claim they are quoting from their speaker and seem pleased with the controversy raised.*

Colleagues, as a scholar of rhetoric and writing and as a critical pedagogue, I am deeply invested in working with students on developing the skills, strategies, and habits of mind to voice their opinions, to enter into serious debate with others, to engage in acts of provocation that alert us to their concerns and issues. I am proud of the work I do here, and I feel privileged to work with smart students who challenge me every day.

I am not challenged by this sign. I am damaged by it. I grew up in the Deep South, where I struggled to form a healthy iden-

tity as a gay man. It's just not that I knew I was different. I was told repeatedly — by friends, family, church members, and my school — that homosexuality was a sin that deserved eternal punishment. I nearly committed suicide in my early 20s after hearing such condemnation for most of my life. My family was poor, but I eventually educated myself to the point where I could leave on my own terms and make a life for myself elsewhere. My husband and I now live in California, where we are (fortunately) rarely assaulted by signs, much less verbal or physical actions, that call for the punishment of faggots.

Obviously, we live in a world in which people hold different opinions about a range of topics. Some believe that people of African descent are intellectually inferior. Others believe that Latinos are lazy and should be kept out of our country. And some believe LGBT people are dangerous and should be punished. While we might believe such views are wrong, we hope that continued conversation will enlighten. Such conversations can be challenging, even provoking. I've had many of them in my nearly 50 years of life on this planet. What concerns me is less that students might hold these views, but that they thought it perfectly acceptable to ask their question — which isn't identified as a quotation on the poster — and that the campus didn't think it might be injurious to other students, staff, and faculty. Surely, let's have the discussion about homosexuality they want to have. But while I am walking to work, do I and others need to have that question framed as an assault on our lives, with words of hate?

Do I need to be reminded of the fragile young man I was, assaulted not just by bullies but by whole systems and institutions of thought that would have rather seen me burn in hell than find another man to love? I don't need that reminder; I live with the memories of that young man every day.

Others on our campus live with similar memories. Despite gains in rights for LGBT people, homophobia and transphobia remain pressing problems for many in our society. And while we are fortunate to live in a relatively tolerant state, others in the country aren't. We have many conversations ahead of us. I hope they can begin from a place that recognizes our shared humanity.

This sign does not recognize my humanity. It de-humanizes me.
I do not want these students punished. They are here to learn.
I hope you will agree that this is a teachable moment, that there is
an opportunity here to help these students and others on campus
consider further the kinds of debates about issues that we want to
have. These students want to provoke; I understand that. But a
provocation that dehumanizes shuts conversation down. It might
also further damage others who are struggling, like I did, with
their sexual identity. I thought of those students all weekend long,
so I am writing you now so you can think about them too.[7]

***

---

7 I *did* send this to my chancellor and provost at the time. There was no response.

I'm writing this the Monday morning after a global summit at Vatican City, in which the Catholic Church has brought together priests, cardinals, laypeople, and the abused from around the world to discuss next steps in addressing catholic priests' abuse of children. The summit ends, and the primary demands of the abused — those willing to come forward to confront the institution that often refused to acknowledge the abuse, and in some cases, in all too many cases, covered up the abuse — remain unmet. The abused wanted the Pope to declare without reservation that priests who abuse children and those priests who cover up such abuse will be defrocked, severed from the Church. Such seems a simple, straightforward request. No tolerance for those who abuse children, for those who condone such abuse by hiding it.

But no, the abused do not get what they want. There will be no such declaration.

Not now, not yet.

***

My last memory of my uncle is visiting him while he lay on his deathbed, in a hospital in New Orleans that no longer exists, curiously enough the hospital in which I'd been born. His brothers and sisters and some nephews and nieces were all in from out of town, converging on death, assembling in the time of crisis, the kind of family that, whatever its many other faults, is at least present in times of trouble.

At the time, I was twelve, maybe thirteen. My mother took me in to see Glen as he fought for his last breaths in the intensive care unit. Only a couple of people were allowed in at a time. He was barely able to sit up, but perhaps I'm misremembering this, perhaps he was fully reclined. But I remember his struggle to breathe, the painfully quick and shallow breaths. I remember the fear, the darting eyes, the look of panic, the pale skin, the bare scalp, all of the signs of someone looking in the face of death, seeing his own death quickly approaching, and not wanting it, desperately not wanting it. Really, though, I don't know how much of this is real, how much of this I'm remembering or misremembering or making up.

But the images of him, breathing in panic, the darting eyes — those are with me; they have been with me for decades, real or not. The images. I have no recollection of what I might have felt, if anything at all. What can someone who is only twelve years old know of such things?

Perhaps I knew enough to have pity, to feel sorry, to not hold much against him, including his leaving, his leaving, his imminent departure, and what would be taken from my life, an uncle, a gay uncle, someone who might have known what I was about to go through, what I was about to feel — even if he had possibly abused me as a child. Surely I couldn't have known that or been thinking about such things at the time. If I was, I have no recollection of doing so at all. But who knows what a twelve year old knows, or remembers, or felt, or could feel, at such a time, in such a place? When I think back, I just see myself, unknowing, but looking at him, a panicked man, unknowing of what lay ahead, panicked because he knew all too well that he would not rise from that bed.

I don't know. What can any of us know of such things until we approach our final hours? But the panic, his panic, his fear, his palpable fear — I remember, whether real or not.

***

With everything that's gone before, with all I've said, I find myself delighting in my capacity to experience surprise. The grooves of damage and resentment aren't the only paths along which I tread. There are detours, further deviations, the unexpected. Surprises — not the least of which has been unexpectedly becoming the object, at my advanced age, of some sexual interest. I'm not bragging. I have found the experience largely amusing, perhaps even a bit unsettling. (But perhaps he protests too much, you might think. We'll get back to that.)

Yes, an unusual experience, for many reasons. I have been a very unconventional looking gay man for the majority of my life. My head is large, my ears protrude, my eyes cross, and my paunch wages a constant battle with my inner thin man for control of my somatic psyche. I am not, given the particular standards and values of the gay community, a looker. I do not recognize myself in our glossy magazines or on the television shows that desperately pitch gay stereotypes, however gorgeous, to a public looking for decorating tips. But I've held my own, now married with my partner of over twenty years. And I go to the gym regularly, but not because one of my closest friends, another middle-aged gay guy, says I should. I will never have a slim figure; my teen twink days are long gone, and I won't do what it takes to get them back, no matter how over-valued such a body type is among some gay men. Instead, I will always be something of a bear (a larger hairy gay man, for those not in the know). And I'm good with that. I exercise to keep myself flexible, for, as we age, the body tightens, the joints wanting to solidify. I'm not done yet, I tell my body — *keep moving.*

I have learned to love my crossed eye.

Other people seem okay with it too, or at least I surmise as such from the uptick in interest I'm experiencing. At first, it startled me, the somewhat blatant commenting on my body at the gym, such as a middle-aged woman's frank interest. "Hey, that's a heavy weight — you're making great progress!… Hey, looking good!… Hey, I'm keeping my eye on you!" I didn't know how to respond so am afraid I came across as dismissive. "Oh, thanks," I muttered as I returned to my bicep curl. But really, I was more perplexed than anything. And then the even stranger come-ons from *young men,* at times actively pursuing conversation at, say, my hipster barbershop, then asking for my name while perusing my body up and down, giving me a good old-fashioned look over.

But perhaps the biggest surprise came when, lounging in the sauna one evening after a workout at my gym, a young shirtless blond kid started cruising me. I say "kid" for he must've been in his early twenties, so a kid to me. But he was a hot kid. Slightly tanned, very toned, his sauna-induced sweat riding the curves of his muscles, wending its way down valleys left vacant by the readily apparent absence of fat. We were alone in the sauna, and he started pacing a bit, periodically catching my eye. Sauna etiquette — in this mixed-gender, suburban gym — dictates that I turn away, look elsewhere, study my fingernails, and I did, but he was hard not to eye aslant; he was just that good-looking. And then he started doing push-ups, balancing himself on a wooden bench, the push-ups intensifying as he propelled himself off the bench to clap his hands and then back down again, pressing himself into the wood. He flexed his taut buttocks, the fabric of his silver shorts perfectly cupping his glutes. Then another sideways glance, just to see if I'm looking. How could I not? He was clearly performing for me. And then he flipped over, supporting himself on his palms, his obvious erection filling the front of his shorts.

At that point someone else walked into the sauna, a middle-aged Asian woman who took a seat and studied her lap. The boy moved over and commenced flexing his muscles practically in front of my face. Eventually, recognizing perhaps that I wasn't taking the bait, he grabbed his towel and walked out, but not before a quick backward glance.

Telling this story to others, I have called this scene one of "being cruised," though, to be completely fair, I cannot tell exactly what this young man's intentions were. I've seen many men flex their muscles in the sauna. Hell, I've done that myself, though always with my shirt on. Perhaps he was just enjoying the heat, getting in a little extra exercise, working up a bit more than the usual sweat. He may not have wanted to engage me sexually at all, or perhaps he just wanted to show off a bit and enjoy some attention. Some people enjoy being watched. Then again, if I had commented, perhaps he would've been repulsed. Maybe he wasn't thinking of me at all, and any interaction with me would've been not only unwanted but a cause for alarm on his part. When I related this story to my husband, he was adamant: "No, you were being cruised. That kid wanted some daddy action." But maybe this is my husband's own projection, his attraction to me now vectored through my story of this hot young man showing off his muscles in the sauna.

This is the challenge of cruising. What *did* he want, if anything? Or is the interest all in my own head? Certainly I was intrigued. Perhaps I'm not used to the protocols of cruising and don't know how to read the cues, and I am now *misreading* the cues, or reading *into* the cues, which aren't even cues at all. I certainly have little experience in responding to them positively; I am unpracticed in casual sex.

But I would be lying if I said that the scene wasn't a little bit exciting. I'm coming to enjoy being looked at, having spent so much of my life oblivious to the potentially erotic interest of strangers, driven as I was by my own homophobia-fueled sense of my unattractiveness and being unwanted. It is, to the say the least, a delightful change of somatic pace to find myself... of interest.

It's also a little bit frightening, in part because I don't always know what's going on. I sense the interest, but don't know how to decline it politely. I've been married too long, off the market, out of circulation. But I also recognize — more profoundly — the gaping hole left by our fundamental inability to interpret someone else's intentions. Take the kid in the sauna, for instance. I was intrigued but also a bit scared. He's flexing, pumping his body, prowling that small wooden room. He seems, at points, frankly dangerous, his young animal body caught in a cage, looking for an out. The presence of the Asian woman intensified my inability to "read" this situation. We're in a shared, mixed-gender public space, so the "cues" are harder for me to interpret.

I couldn't help but think about what she must have been think-ing of this young stud, sexually charging this tiny space with his gyrations, his cock on display. And perhaps that's yet another twist: the young stud might be enjoying teasing me a bit *in the presence of yet a third person,* who can observe this little silent drama unfolding.

The drama, such as it is, occurs almost entirely in these varied invitations to look and the exchanges of looks that generate ten-sion because they are not being interpreted or clarified through verbal articulation. I sneak a look at the boy who catches my eye who catches me watching him while another watches. Just looking opens up a world of possibility. Looking is all potential.

One of the most startling scenes of the power of looking occurs for me in Michelangelo Antonioni's 1960 masterpiece, *L'Avventura,* in which our heroine, Claudia, helping her love in-terest track down a missing friend, finds herself in a square in a strange city. A crowd of men gather around her, following her, their sexual hunger palpable in their eyes. No doubt, the young Monica Vitti was worth looking at, but the scene is overplayed, purposefully so. The lovers are searching for their companion, a search reflected more basely in the searching eyes of the men practically stalking Claudia. The scene is a study in the male gaze, a disturbing invitation itself to gaze at that gaze, to be un-settled by it.[8]

Such a scene likely prompted theorist Roland Barthes, in his 1980 letter, "Dear Antonioni," to meditate on the power of the gaze, and the ways in which artists like Antonioni proffer invitations to reflect on how we look at the world around us, and at one another. Barthes suggests that an "aspect of fragility for the artist, paradoxically, is the firmness and insistence of his look. Power of any kind, because it is violence, never looks; if it looked one minute longer (one minute too much) it would lose its essence as power. The artist, for his part, stops and looks

---

8   *L'Avventura* was originally released in 1960 and the Criterion Collection, unsurprisingly, has a lovely edition of it.

lengthily."[9] Barthes understood that much atrocity and violence has likely been committed because perpetrators haven't bothered to look carefully enough at what they were doing, whom they were harming, how their actions were damaging others. If they looked steadily at the suffering they were causing, would they continue? How much pain has been caused by our willingness to, as we say, turn a blind eye? What suffering is furthered when we turn away from misery? What terrible power is enacted by not looking closely enough at what we are doing? In *L'Avventura*, the men are watching Claudia, but they aren't looking *at her*. They aren't seeing *her*. They see an attractive woman, but not the person herself on a quest, searching, grappling with the complexities of friendship, intimacy, and love.

Some of us are subject to gazes that size us up, measure us, and invite us to internalize such measuring. As you know by now, I grew up with such gazes, my thin and gangly body, coupled with my somewhat effeminate mannerisms, lured the hostile gazes of jocks and bullies throughout my schooling. Taunts, ridicule, homophobic labeling, the silent condoning of such by adults — all tying the deep braid among body, identity, and eroticism into a dense knot of self-hatred that has taken me most of my life to untangle. People were definitely looking at me, but they weren't seeing the damage they were inflicting — or they didn't care. So no wonder that, years later, personal success and overgrowth aside, I still react skeptically to interest in my *body*. "Who, what, me? I don't think so." I was trained early on to expect that the most my body could elicit in others is castigation and punishment, not interest, much less desire.

But I think Barthes didn't quite see the whole picture in that scene in *L'Avventura*. Yes, it's a bit disturbing, the male gaze creepily intensifying as more men join the throng tracking Claudia through the square. But Claudia moves through

---

9   The text of Barthes's letter to Antonioni can be found online here: http://shihlun.blogspot.com/2015/07/dear-antonioni-roland-barthes-1980.html. My quotations come from page 67 of the letter as published in *L'Avventura* by Geoffrey Nowell-Smith.

them without comment, as though she's not even noticing them noticing her. Perhaps she's naïvely unaware of the danger she might be in. Perhaps she's secretly delighting in it. Perhaps she just understands it as her due as an attractive woman. The power of the scene might ultimately lie in the presence of intense looking that generates dramatic tension without resolving it.

So, thinking through this scene, I now recognize that I wasn't entirely truthful earlier. Surely, I go to the gym because, as a gay man in the greater Los Angeles area, I don't want to be fat. Even though I'm not "on the market" and am happily married, I've nonetheless internalized some somatic sensibility about what a normative gay body looks like. One might call this the Foucauldian panopticon in operation, working at the level of a gay community policing its bodies to impose standards of attractiveness. But I might also understand my own attention to my body as a desire to proliferate the possibilities for looking. I want to be cruised. I desire the desiring gazes of others. In part, I'm working against the narrative of looking that I learned as a kid: that the only gaze I deserve is one of hostility. I want now a different narrative, an expanded set of possibilities.

Without a doubt, there are some exercises of power that stem from a conscious failure to look closely enough, that elide the human subject and suffering in the execution of violence on other bodies. I forced myself to listen to the daily news report of the trial and sentencing of Larry Nassar. I wouldn't turn away from hearing the awful details as one woman after another came forward to speak of their abuse. I felt a human obligation to bear witness, even from afar, to what happens when someone fails to see the human before him, and sees instead a tool for his gratification.

If I return to that sauna room, I also see the operations of looking and power at play… but not in any simple way. The boy seemed to be presenting his finely sculpted body for objectification, wanting to be looked at, his shirtless torso admired, his gluteal globes pulsing with his push-ups. I have a hard time imagining that one flexes and grunts in a sauna, nearly naked, without some desire to be appreciated. However, in the absence of a clear invitation ("Hey, do you want to touch my taut ass?"), how am I to read his body, his performance, even his glances at me? Is he just checking to see if I'm looking, and might he be thinking something more vicious, less invitational? Something like, *Why is this old faggot staring at me?* And maybe he's right to think that. Maybe in looking at him, however furtively, and then again in writing about him here, I'm contributing to the objectification of his body, delighting in my adjectival portraiture of his form, and thus failing to see him as a person.

But no. I *am* trying to imagine what he might be thinking, to sift through the possibilities of perception, not just in my mind but in his as well. And even further, I'm trying to imagine what's going on in the mind of the woman who joins the scene, walking into this silent drama, this unspoken narrative. I'm trying to imagine what she too is thinking and feeling, how she might be experiencing his dance, and my silence.

Part of the thrill of such situations lies precisely in the speculation, in the possibility that, if I were to make a move on this boy, I could be wrong in my interpretation. Moreover, all of this speculation is embedded in a public space, where I'm perhaps not supposed to be acknowledging or responding to (much less initiating) sexual contact. That's part of the excitement. The erotic charge is built on the dual unknowability and illicit nature of the space. Indeed, without articulating our sense of what's going on, how can I know what someone else is thinking or feeling or wanting or desiring — provided, of course, that they will be truthful in the telling of their own needs and wishes?

Herein lies the complexity of cruising and being cruised. Cruising implies that we are just passing through, looking around, checking stuff out, window-shopping as it were. Will we or won't we? Even if we are the ones doing the cruising, we might not ourselves fully know what we are looking for. Part of the pleasure comes out of the play of possibility, not always the follow-through.

We want to look, and we want to be looked at. We want interest, and we want to be interested in others. There can even be some fun in being objectified; I know that I haven't minded some appreciative appraisals, even if the interaction stops there. I can be someone's gay daddy, even if just in his own mind. I value such fantasy. I am surprised at times how much of waking life is composed of moving through spaces with the drama of the possible permeating how I see the world around me and interact with people and things in it.

At the same time, as delightful as such play is, we must always be conscious of how such looking and interest carry with them the limitations of our own perceptions. All of our eyes are a bit crossed. We don't always know how the other will understand our actions, our words, our gyrations in the sauna room, our looks askance, our stroll through a crowded square — or our gazes on someone else moving through that square. But just at the moment when we are paying such necessary attention to what is appropriate and not when we look, desire, and might want to reach out and touch, when we are becoming more conscious of how we see and sometimes objectify one another, I hope we can leave some room for cruising.

Being cruised has been, for me, strangely but deliciously reparative. I didn't realize that I needed that scene in the sauna room, even as I needed to meditate on it, even as I may have needed to pick up my towel and walk away.

***

I only realize later, much later, that the film I dreamed of— *We Are Only*— not the film itself (which I never see in the dream; I'm always only in the lobby, the theatrical waiting room), but the title, the title itself, could be a note from the subconscious, the unconscious, whatever it is that shadows the more conscious narrative we tell ourselves

We are only; *we're lonely.*

Funny how the mind works like that, punning, cunning in its wordplay. I so much as a child and young man had to depend on myself, find the resources or create them (as we say) to survive my life. *One, only.*

But also, therefore, lonely.

But also, therefore, "we," the creative we that the mind populates to counter the many wes given to one by the others, the many wes that whisper constantly to one about how lonely you are. But also, therefore, not lonely, not *only.*

Who is that *we*? Who are they, if not all of the voices inside, implanted and generated— given, received, countered, retold, shaped into other utterances?

All of the voices, all of the only, lonely voices.

Works Cited

Antonioni, Michaelangelo, dir. *L'Avventura*. Cino Del Duca, 1960.

Barthes, Roland. "Dear Antonioni (1980)." 影印班長, July 12, 2015. http://shihlun.blogspot.com/2015/07/dear-antonioni-roland-barthes-1980.html.

Berger, Edward, dir. *Patrick Melrose*. Showtime, May 12–June 9, 2018.

Dollimore, Jonathan. *Sexual Dissidence: Augustine to Freud, Wilde to Foucault*. Oxford: Oxford University Press, 1991.

Downen, Robert, Lise Olsen, and John Tedesco. "Abuse of Faith." *Houston Chronicle,* February 10, 2019. https://www.houstonchronicle.com/news/investigations/article/Southern-Baptist-sexual-abuse-spreads-as-leaders-13588038.php.

Gaither Music TV. "Michael W. Smith - Friends (Live)." *YouTube,* September 25, 2015. https://www.youtube.com/watch?v=SAeD2UEYaAk.

Huxley, Aldous. *The Doors of Perception*. New York: Harper and Row, 1954.

Leitch, David, dir. *Deadpool 2*. 20th Century Fox, Marvel Entertainment, 2018.

Lennox, Annie. "Why." *Diva*, Arista, 1992.

Lorde, Audre. "A Litany for Survival." *Poetry Foundation.*
    https://www.poetryfoundation.org/poems/147275/a-litany-
    for-survival.
Maxwell, William. *The Folded Leaf.* New York: Harper, 1945.
Miller, Tim, dir. *Deadpool.* 20th Century Fox, Marvel
    Entertainment, 2016.
Nowell-Smith, Geoffrey. *L'Avventura.* London: BFI, 1997.

Pollan, Michael. *How to Change Your Mind: What the New
    Science of Psychedelics Teaches Us About Consciousness,
    Dying, Addiction, Depression, and Transcendence.* New York:
    Penguin Books, 2019.
Rimbaud, Arthur. *Complete Works, Selected Letters.* Translated
    by Wallace Fowlie. Chicago: University of Chicago Press,
    1966.
Sebold, Alice. *Lucky.* New York: Scribner, 1999.
Silverblatt, Michael. "Eileen Myles: Evolution." *Bookworm,*
    KCRW, Santa Monica, November 8, 2018.
Smith, Michael W. "Awesome God." *YouTube,* November 5,
    2014. https://www.youtube.com/watch?v=d2orOoIX3nM.
St. Aubyn, Edward. *The Patrick Melrose Novels.* New York:
    Picador, 2012.
Sturridge, Charles, and Michael Lindsay-Hogg, dir. *Brideshead
    Revisited.* Granada Television, October 12–December 22,
    1981.
Waugh, Evelyn. *Brideshead Revisited: The Sacred and Profane
    Memories of Captain Charles Ryder. A Novel.* London:
    Chapman & Hall Ltd., 1945.
White, Edmund. *Rimbaud: The Double Life of a Rebel.*
    Bloomsbury: Atlantic, 2009.

Made in the USA
Monee, IL
07 November 2021